Thomas A. Simonds, S.J., Ed.D. and

WRITING A NEW STORY for Catholic Schools

Published in the United States of America by the National Catholic Educational Association.

www.NCEA.org

ISBN 978-1-55833-753-4
Part No. ADM-31-1632

TABLE OF CONTENTS

ACKNOWLEDGEMENTS

We gratefully acknowledge the work of The Center for Catholic School Effectiveness, School of Education, Loyola University Chicago, and the Barbara and Patrick Roche Center for Catholic Education, Lynch School of Education, Boston College, for developing ***The National Standards and Benchmarks for Effective Catholic Elementary and Secondary Schools***. The National Standards and Benchmarks are utilized in this book as a guide and resource for educators who engage in the process of writing a new story of success for their schools.

Some material in Chapters One through Four previously appeared as articles in a series written by Fr. Simonds and published by the National Catholic Educational Association in Momentum between 2015 and 2018.

Web materials and social media materials from schools included in Chapter Six are used with permission.

We are thankful to Jerry Meyer who assisted with research on regional and network Catholic schools. We are also thankful to Creighton University for supporting this project.

Imprimi Potest

Imprimi Potest

May 21, 2021

Rev. Glen Chun, S.J.

Assistant Provincial

Midwest Province

Society of Jesus

PREFACE TO PART ONE

Imagine that God gave you an extraordinary pen and the opportunity to write a new success story for the Catholic schools of the future. What would you write? What is the very best you can imagine and hope for the Catholic schools of tomorrow?

As you ponder what you might write, let me introduce the focus of this book. I propose that we can write a new success story for Catholic schools by adapting important lessons from the past to take strategic and unified action now and in the future. My bold proposal provides detailed information about how to take the steps necessary to implement new ideas and strategies for success. This book can be used by leaders, parents, and supporters of Catholic schools at all levels from pre-school through grade twelve in the United States of America. Leaders and stakeholders starting a new Catholic school will also find this book helpful.

I firmly believe that the proposal I share in this book will be a game-changer for Catholic schools if groups of committed people accept my proposal and act on it. My proposal is based on two key drivers that led to a national enrollment in Catholic schools of 5.2 million students (McDonald & Schultz, 2020, p. 2). Keep in mind that the national enrollment in Catholic schools is now around 1.7 million students, approximately the same number of students as in home schools (McDonald & Schultz, 2020, p. 2; NCES, 2019, Table 206.10).

Two Key Drivers of School Success

In Chapter One, I briefly review the history of Catholic schools in the United States of America in order to elucidate the three key drivers of enrollment success prior to the Second Vatican Council: affordability, broad support, and networking. In Chapters Two through Four, I explain how you can apply the principles of affordability, broad support, and networking to write a new success story for your Catholic school.

In Chapters Five and Six, my co-author, Ron Fussell, will describe for you how to apply my proposal for success to your Catholic school. Ron will address the issue of hiring faculty in Chapter Five, and he will address best practices in school communications in Chapter Six.

Indexing to National Standards

The ideas and strategies that make up my proposal are indexed to the *National Standards and Benchmarks for Effective Catholic Elementary and Secondary Schools* (NSBECS) (Ozar & Weitzel-O'Neill, 2012). Benchmarks for success are provided at the beginning of

Chapters Two through Six along with a website for more information. The benchmarks are discussed in each chapter to flesh out how to successfully implement the ideas and strategies in this book at your Catholic school.

PART ONE

Writing a New Success Story for Your Catholic School

Thomas A. Simonds, S.J., Ed.D.

CHAPTER ONE:
A Proposal for Success

To write a new story for Catholic schools, we first need to understand the old story of Catholic schools in the United States of America. A focused review of the history of Catholic schools will enable us to identify key drivers of enrollment success that we can adapt and use to write a new success story today. As we look through our past, we will discover something unsavory: elements of the anti-Catholicism that have continued to have a negative impact on Catholic schools into the 21st century.

Catholics in a Protestant Nation Needed Their Own Schools

The story of Catholic schools begins with the story of our nation. When the Thirteen Colonies came together in 1776 to declare their independence from England, the population was primarily Christian and Protestant. Catholics numbered just 25,000 or 1 percent in a total colonial population of 2.5 million (LeBeau, 2000, pp. 61 & 96). Since Protestants made up the bulk of citizens at that time, the books used to teach English to children were also used to teach Protestant religious doctrine.

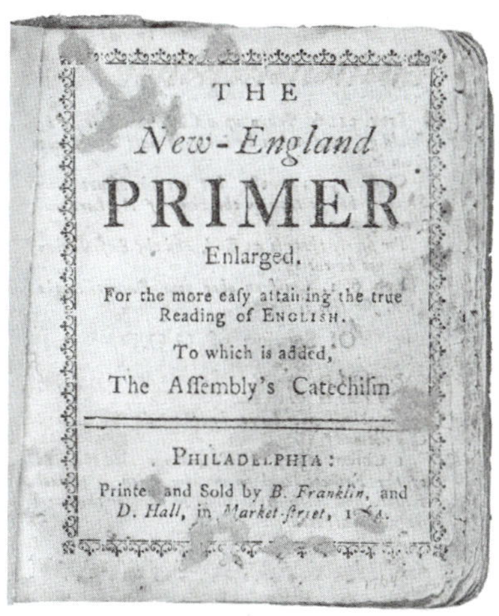

THE

New-England

PRIMER

Enlarged.

For the more eaſy attaining the true Reading of ENGLISH.

To which is added,

The Aſſembly's Catechiſm.

PHILADELPHIA:

Printed and Sold by *B. Franklin*, and *D. Hall*, in *Market-ſtreet*, 1[illegible]4.

The New England Primer, circa 1764

The New England Primer was the most popular text used by children to learn how to read the English language between 1687 and 1800 as noted by Ford (1897/1962): "For one hundred years this Primer was the schoolbook of . . . America, and for another hundred, it was frequently reprinted" (p. 19). *The New England Primer* included a variety of strategies for language acquisition, and also included a short question and answer Puritan catechism. The instructional material, unfortunately, included anti-Catholic content.

John Rogers
(c. 1505 – 4 February 1555)

For example, a picture of a man and his family being burned at the stake in England was included in the 1727 edition of the Primer (Ford, 1897/1962, p. 88). Below the picture, a text was inserted that explained that Mr. John Rodgers, a Protestant minister, along with his family, were being burned at the stake for their Protestant beliefs by Queen Mary of England, who was Catholic. An exhortation that followed the picture and was attributed to John Rodgers included these lines:

> Abhor that arrant Whore of Rome,
> and all her Blasphemies;
> And drink not of her cursed Cup,
> obey not her decrees. (Ford, 1897/1962, p. 90)

Later editions of the Primer included a picture of the Catholic pope, who was described for children as "the Pope, or man of sin" (Ford, 1897/1962, p. 50). These examples from a facsimile of the 1727 edition of *The New England Primer*, and from the introduction to the facsimile copy of the Primer by Ford published in 1897, demonstrate that American children were being taught anti-Catholic sentiments from a very young age when our nation was founded.

However, while the farmers, laborers, and shopkeepers were strictly religious and brought their children up to be like themselves, other people during the 1700s had a much more liberal view of religious belief. Thomas Jefferson and Benjamin Franklin were proponents of the Enlightenment tenets that strict sectarian religion was antithetical to true wisdom and understanding, which could best be attained using human reason and the scientific method. Jefferson, Franklin, and other proponents of these ideas thought that God had created the world and set it on its course with no further thought or care about us or the world he had created. For thinkers in the Enlightenment tradition, it was up to the human person using reason and skill to make progress and advance what God had begun.

Enlightenment thinkers characterized the Catholic religion as a deceitful plot contrived by the pope and priests to maintain power by keeping all people in darkness and ignorance. Thus, in addition to the anti-Catholic beliefs being taught to children during the 1700s, the hugely influential principles of the Enlightenment also created an anti-Catholic sentiment among the leaders and thinkers of this time period.

Of course, the principal focus of Jefferson, Franklin, and all the leaders of the American Revolution was to create a new nation. Jefferson, Benjamin Rush, Noah Webster and other influential thinkers and leaders thought that a common school experience for all children of the fledgling nation would be the most important means of creating a common American culture.

Horace Mann, thought of as the founder of public schools, or common schools as they were called at that time, took up the banner of free schools for all in 1837 and promoted common schools for all children between the ages of four and 16 in the Commonwealth of Massachusetts (Cremin, 1979, p. 30). Because Mann thought that one school for all children was critical for advancing American democracy through a shared experience of education, he advocated for a common Christianity in the common schools that would bring all students, parents, and educators together in a common cause. This common Christianity, as Mann saw it, was made up of the common beliefs of all Christians, but in fact, the common school Christianity focused on the Protestant version of Christianity which the majority of Americans practiced at that time.

Horace Mann (1796-1859)

This common Christianity, which became part of the curriculum of the common school and was included in the McGuffey Readers, was an acceptable compromise for a time (Gorn, 1998). But when large numbers of Catholic immigrants arrived in the United States of America beginning in the mid-1800s and continuing into the early 1900s, religious tensions developed. The original, mostly Protestant immigrants to the United States of America, who now saw themselves as the natives, believed that one nation needed one language, one religion, and one common culture to grow and develop. The odd cultural ways, different religions, and different languages of new immigrant groups were seen as problematic by the self-styled nativist thinkers. The solution developed by the nativists was to Americanize all immigrants through the common schools.

Horace Mann described the negative effects of Catholic and all sectarian schools and the need for common schools in his 1837 report to the Massachusetts board of public education. Mann wrote,

> Amongst any people, sufficiently advanced in intelligence, to perceive, that hereditary opinions on religious subjects are not always coincident with truth, it cannot be overlooked, that the tendency of the private school system is to assimilate our modes of education to those of England, where churchmen and dissenters,– each sect according to its own creed,– maintain separate schools, in which children are taught, from their tenderest years to wield the sword of polemics with fatal dexterity; and where the gospel, instead of being a temple of peace, is converted into an armory of deadly weapons, for social, interminable warfare. Of such disastrous consequences, there is but one remedy and one preventive. It is the elevation of the common schools. (Cremin, 1979, p. 33)

While it is true that Horace Mann advocated for a groundswell of support that would bring everyone running to the common schools instead of draconian measures such as closing private schools and requiring children to attend the common schools, his line of thinking certainly did not allow for any compromise with Catholics or other non-Protestants, such as those of the Jewish faith. As we will soon understand, when Catholics did not naturally gravitate to the common schools, nativists eventually did seek to take draconian measures against Catholics and Catholic schools.

Attacks Mounted Against Catholic Schools

As the number of Catholics swelled in the United States in the late 1800s and early 1900s, Catholics began to build their own separate schools so that they could pass on their culture and faith to their children while also preparing their children to live and work in a democratic nation. Catholics had to pay for each school that was built, as leaders in government at that time saw a separate school system as antithetical to the needs of the nation.

Sentiments against Catholic schools ran so strong that in the 1870s, President Grant and Congressman James Blaine advocated for an amendment to the U.S. Constitution that would have prevented any federal or state tax dollars from being given to any private school. The proposed amendment passed in the House of Representatives but was eventually defeated in the Senate.

But that did not end the matter. Feeling strongly that one common school system operated by local governments was the best means to instill a common set of values in all citizens, advocates of the Blaine Amendment worked to insert similar language in the constitutions of the various states. Subsequently, 37 states adopted versions of the Blaine Amendment in their state constitutions. Through the Blaine Amendment process, Catholics were given the message that if they wanted their own schools, they would have to shoulder the costs themselves.

Making Catholic Schools Affordable

In Catholic circles, the need for separate Catholic schools became a social force of great power. A groundswell of support for Catholic schools resulted in new Church pronouncements about the importance of such schools as well as the start on construction of what would become an impressive network of local school systems. But back in the 1800s, the challenge that had to be met was the cost not only of building each school but also the cost of operating each school.

Bishops, pastors, and families worked together to build school buildings to address the need for separate schools that were culturally and religiously appropriate for Catholic children. Bishops and pastors sought out religious priests, brothers, and sisters to staff these new schools. Diocesan priests and the religious priests, brothers, and sisters provided the labor force for these schools at very little cost, creating a living endowment for the schools, with the religious sisters by far making the greatest contribution. The felt need for the schools and for religious and priests to staff the schools helped to support a surge in religious vocations throughout the early and middle parts of the 20th century in the United States, which continually renewed the living endowment of each school.

New Attacks Mounted Against Catholic Schools

Even as Catholics were sacrificing to build their own schools, nativist leaders mounted a new and much stronger attack on Catholic schools by drafting a law in Oregon that would have required all children to attend schools operated by local governments. The argument that one common school was necessary to develop one common American culture and religious tradition was once again trotted out. However, Governor Pierce of Oregon was sued in court by two private schools to prevent the potential law from taking effect. The case eventually made its way to the Supreme Court of the United States of America. In *Pierce v. Society of Sisters* (268 US 510, 1925), nativists lost their bid to destroy Catholic schools. The Supreme Court wrote, "We think it entirely plain that the Act of 1922 unreasonably interferes with the liberty of parents and guardians to direct the upbringing and education of children" (*Pierce v. Society of Sisters*, 268 US 510, 1925).

Given that nativists used a state-by-state strategy to insert Blaine Amendment language in state constitutions, it is highly likely that if the Supreme Court had sided with the governor of Oregon in 1925, other states would have followed Oregon's lead, and the many Catholic schools that had already been built in states across the nation would have been shuttered, never to open again. This close call for the survival of Catholic schools in the United States of America makes it clear just how strong the anti-Catholic and anti-immigrant feelings were among nativists.

But despite the challenges from the nativists, by 1965, 5.2 million Catholic children and youth were enrolled in Catholic schools (McDonald & Schultz, 2020, p. 2). Catholics got what they wanted, a separate system of schools in which children would learn the Catholic faith and be prepared for leadership and employment after graduation.

Loss of Broad Support & Reduced Affordability Lead to Sharp Enrollment Declines

As the 20th century progressed and overt hostility towards Catholics in American society decreased, so did the perceived need for a separate Catholic school system in the United States. Catholics became well educated through their network of Catholic schools, which also included Catholic colleges and universities, and they began to move out of their separate social enclave into the professions and American society. This move of Catholics into the mainstream cultural and social groups within the United States was accelerated by the huge social changes wrought by the Second World War. Catholics traveled to other countries, worked alongside fellow Americans of differing religious affiliations, and saw themselves as patriots serving their country. As Catholics came to be accepted in broader American society, the need for separate schools became less evident to Catholic parents. Their children were welcomed in the local tax-supported schools and the instructional texts had long since dropped overt anti-Catholic references. Catholics were no longer immigrants but had become native-born citizens.

The Catholic Church was also changing her views about society and culture. These changing views among Church leaders and faithful Catholics culminated in the mid-1960s with the publication of the decrees of the Second Vatican Council. The Church opened up to broader involvement in American culture, politics, and institutions. As the threat of anti-Catholicism waned, even some bishops and priests began to question the need for separate Catholic schools in the United States. As the perceived need for Catholic schools continued to decrease so did the number of religious and priests. This decline in religious and priests meant that the living endowment that had supported the education of hundreds of millions of children for more than a century was becoming insufficient to meet the budgetary needs of the now expansive network of local Catholic schools.

To replace the religious and priests that had staffed the schools, pastors began to hire lay men and women to teach in the schools. This move created a necessary and significant increase in school budgets. As costs to families and parishes increased, and parents began to see the tax-supported schools as an option for their children, enrollment in Catholic schools began to quickly decline. As Catholics witnessed a continual decline in the number of priests and religious teaching in the schools, questions began to surface about the unique value proposition that Catholic schools had provided. Parents wondered how a strong Catholic identity could be maintained in the schools with virtually zero priests and religious teaching in the schools.

To address declining enrollments and also to address felt needs for school improvement, Catholic educators have taken steps to ensure the Catholic identity of their schools. Numerous programs, books, and conferences designed to assist Catholic school personnel with learning about and implementing the Catholic pedagogical paradigm have emerged in the years following the Second Vatican Council. However, the Catholic community has not been able to adequately address the financial challenges being faced by PK-12 Catholic schools in the United States.

A Proposal for Success

In Chapters Two and Three, I share my proposal for addressing the issue of affordability of Catholic schools. When Catholic schools were affordable in the past, enrollments were strong. Working together to write a new story for Catholic schools, we can rebuild strong enrollments in Catholic schools through adopting new school models that address affordability, through advocating for broad support of private school education from state and federal governments, and through advocating for full parental choice in the education of their children.

In Chapter Four, I share my proposal for how Catholic schools can write a new story by once again meeting the felt needs of parents, bishops, priests, and other important stakeholders. The Catholic schools of the past met a felt need for safe schools for children that were culturally and religiously appropriate. We need to network with parents, clergy, and stakeholders to discover what they would see as drivers of strong enrollments in Catholic schools today.

CHAPTER TWO:
Affordable Schools

NSBECS Benchmarks for Affordable Catholic Schools

10.1 The governing body and leader/leadership team engage in **financial planning** in collaboration with experts in non-profit management and funding.

10.3 Financial plans define revenue sources that include but are not limited to tuition, tuition assistance/scholarships, endowment funds, **local and regional partnerships, public funding, regional cost sharing,** (arch)diocesan and/or religious communities' assistance, foundation gifts, entrepreneurial options and other sources not listed.

See ***www.catholicschoolstandards.org*** for more information.

The Catholic schools of the past were affordable for every family because of the living endowment provided by the priests and religious who taught and led Catholic schools prior to 1970. Today, we must find a new way to make Catholic schools affordable for every family.

A key Supreme Court decision points the way toward affordable Catholic schools in the United States of America. In *Pierce v. Society of Sisters* (268 US 510, 1925), the United States Supreme Court decided that the State of Oregon could not compel all youth to attend schools operated by local governments, stating that parents have the right to choose the type of education and schools that they think are best for their children. However, it is my position that because of the Blaine Amendment language that was successfully inserted in 37 state constitutions, and because of the funding model used in all states for PK-12 education, states have *de facto* been violating the decision in Pierce by requiring citizens to pay both a local school tax and tuition for a private school if they decide to exercise their right to choose.

Therefore, while the Supreme Court justices in the Pierce case were able to envision a country in which all parents have the right to choose where and how to educate their children, in fact, only parents willing and able to pay double for their children's education, or who educate their own children at home while still paying a public school tax, actually have the freedom to choose their child's education. Clearly, we have more work to do in order to make full and fair parental choice in education a reality for all citizens.

There is no doubt that local, state, and federal governments have a legitimate interest in ensuring that all children and youth receive an education that prepares them to participate in the democratic process and become skilled workers and professionals, but what is the compelling government interest in only funding one school system? The compelling interest behind the Blaine Amendments was that Catholic schools were perceived as un-American, as separatist, and as dangerous to civil unity, as I documented in Chapter One of this book. This so-called compelling interest from the past is no longer a compelling government interest because it is unconstitutional as defined in the Pierce case by the United States Supreme Court. However, while the compelling government interest in funding one school system no longer exists, the practice remains.

I think reasonable people today can agree that PK-12 Catholic schools provide considerable benefits to the common good in local communities and in the nation. For example, graduates of Catholic schools have gone on to be leaders, soldiers, professionals, and productive members of the American workforce for over two centuries. Catholic schools today reflect the diversity of American society, enrolling students of other religions and enrolling racially and ethnically diverse students. Catholic schools provide education for citizenship on par with any other type of school and frequently outperform other types of PK-12 schools in terms of graduate success indicators. Therefore, educators who accept my proposal on how to write a new success story for Catholic schools will want to work with a person skilled and knowledgeable in local, state, and federal funding practices who can advocate for the educational rights of parents and guardians who desire to choose the best school for their children.

The process of realizing the full impact of the Supreme Court's decision in Pierce will take time and effort. But the Supreme Court has already provided us with a place to begin this effort. In *Zelman v. Simmons-Harris* (536 US 639, 2002), the United States Supreme Court upheld an Ohio school voucher program that provided vouchers for school costs to parents who then chose a school for their child and applied the voucher to their child's education. While the ruling in Zelman has a limited scope, as it focused on providing effective educational alternatives to students in an underperforming school system, Zelman does provide a starting place to seek realization of the promise to parents of full and fair parental choice in the education of their children envisioned by the court in Pierce. Broader school voucher programs initiated in more recent years in numerous states provide additional stepping stones on the road to full and fair parental choice in the education of their children. Moving forward, the enrollment success driver of school affordability must be pursued by a broad coalition of stakeholders committed to excellent Catholic and private school education and committed to engaging in democratic advocacy.

Financial Planning

In addition to advocacy, financial planning is key to ensuring the long-term affordability of Catholic schools. Experts in financial planning can assist school leaders with locating all available revenue sources and with prudently utilizing existing resources. In fact, effective and helpful financial planners may already be among your school's stakeholders. School board members and parents who work in local businesses and corporations in the area of finance could likely help school leaders with financial planning efforts. Additionally, financial planning organizations with expertise in the non-profit sector can help with the creation of new long-term financial success plans. These financial planning organizations can assist school leaders and school boards with developing balanced budgets, identifying opportunities for growth, and envisioning new sources of revenue.

As each year passes, the array of revenue sources and new success models for Catholic schools continues to increase as stakeholders seek to strengthen Catholic education, but these new sources of revenue and new success models are either not known or are not cultivated widely by leaders in Catholic schools. Therefore, in the following sections of this chapter, I help you start writing your new success story by providing detailed information about a number of new school success models that directly address affordability. For each success model, I provide contact information so you can learn more, a brief history of the initiative, a description of the model, and additional helpful information.

These new models for school organization, governance, and funding have been highly successful. At the same time, I do want to note that there have been some individual instances in which a model has been unsuccessful, leading to the closure of a school or reduction in the number of schools in a network. Because these problems have occurred, I think it is critical to do your homework and talk with organizations who have successfully adopted these new models to ensure that the model you decide to adopt will be successful.

Regional Catholic Schools

Contact Information to Learn More

*Bishop Heelan Catholic Schools, Sioux City, Iowa
https://bishopheelan.org

*Holy Family Catholic Schools, Dubuque, Iowa
https://www.holyfamilydbq.org/

*Siena Catholic Schools, Racine, Wisconsin
https://www.sienacatholicschools.org/

Brief History

The regional school success model began as early as the 1990s as a new means to reduce costs and create a PK-12 Catholic school system in specific cities and areas of (arch) dioceses. Bishop Heelan Catholic Schools in Sioux City, IA, was set up as a regional school system in 1998. Pastors and lay people serve on the regional school board in Sioux City. The regional school success model continues to expand across the country as (arch)dioceses and stakeholders seek out more cost-effective means to operate Catholic schools.

Program Description

Much like a tax-supported school district, a regional Catholic school system has early childhood programs, elementary schools, middle schools, and high schools. Elementary school students matriculate to a larger middle school and then to a high school within the same Catholic school system. Within this success model, then, there is an inbuilt feeder system for student enrollment as students move to grade level schools within the same system.

A regional school board provides oversight and support for individual schools, including professional development for staff, creation and dissemination of policies, facilitation of the relationship with the local (arch)bishop, bulk purchasing of supplies, and fund-raising. Regional schools draw students from a larger geographic region than the traditional parish school. Some individual parish schools may be closed or used only for specific grades in the new regional school model. The economy of scale enables regional schools to operate in a more cost-effective manner. The inbuilt feeder system helps to stabilize enrollment within the school system. Priests assist with religious formation and provide a pastoral presence in the schools. In some regional school models, pastors serve as members of regional school boards.

Marketing

Cost savings and networking opportunities are two marketing points that can be emphasized by regional Catholic school systems. By working with a local education authority (LEA), often a tax-supported school district, regional school boards can advocate for support of transportation of students to regional Catholic schools. So, rather than building new Catholic schools in areas without schools, the regional school model provides a means to utilize existing Catholic school buildings and maximize enrollment within those buildings, thereby saving parents and all stakeholders money. The use of tax-supported school buses and other means of transportation will save parents time and provide more social networking opportunities for students. Students and parents may also become involved in new parts of their cities and regions and develop networks of relationships with people living close to the schools.

Public support of transportation expenses for students who attend private schools has been approved by the United States Supreme Court based on the child benefit concept (*Everson v. Board of Education*, 330 U.S. 1, 1947). The provision of school transportation is a benefit provided to all PK-12 students in specific local areas. Just like fire and police protection, school transportation is a public service. By supporting school transportation, local and state governments provide a secular benefit to support the success of children that does not require government to become entangled with the exercise of religion.

A third focus point for marketing regional Catholic schools is the continuity for students within the system. Rather than having to decide about what school to attend after grade school, students in a regional school can continue within the same school system and maintain their circle of friends. We all are aware of the fact that young people and parents often must make difficult decisions when it comes time to move from a grade school to a high school. Decisions about school attendance made by a child's circle of friends become more important in the upper elementary school grades. The regional school model greatly reduces this stressor for families and young people by providing a natural next step for high school within one continuous school system that spans pre-kindergarten through grade 12.

Network & Consortium Schools

Contact Information to Learn More

*Catholic Partnership Schools, Diocese of Camden, New Jersey
https://www.catholicpartnershipschools.org/

*CUES School System, Archdiocese of Omaha, Nebraska
https://www.cuesschools.org/

*Drexel Schools, Diocese of San Jose, California
https://www.drexel.dsj.org/

*Seton Catholic Schools, Archdiocese of Milwaukee, Wisconsin
https://www.setoncatholicschools.com/

Brief History

The network and consortium school success model began as early as 2008, with the founding of the Catholic Partnership Schools in Camden, NJ. The network school model is proliferating throughout the United States as (arch)dioceses explore new ways to affordably operate Catholic schools while maintaining maximum access to Catholic schools for interested families. The terms network schools and consortium schools both designate a group of schools that are grouped together under one administrator or administrative body.

Program Description

Network schools and consortium schools characteristically are composed of grade schools that are operated by one administrator or administrative group. Often the administrative group is a private, non-profit organization that partners with an (arch)diocese to oversee education within a set of designated schools. Pastors are less likely to be involved in oversight of the schools in this model, and priests assist with religious formation and provide a pastoral presence in the schools.

Existing parish grade schools are grouped together into a network, and oversight of the schools is transferred from the parishes to the network administrative group. Some former parish schools may be closed in order to consolidate and maximize enrollment in the largest and most physically sound school buildings.

Cost reductions in the network school model result from having one administrative group engage in purchasing, oversight, and fund-raising for all the schools in the network. Additional cost savings can be realized by closing small schools and maximizing student enrollment in the most ideal school locations. A contract for services is often entered into by the network administrative group and the (arch)diocese. Stipulations may be included in the contract that allow the (arch)diocese to dissolve the contract in specified circumstances such as poor oversight of the schools or failing enrollments. Advocacy for and agreements with local education agencies (LEAs) to provide transportation for school children can be another important part of the enhanced affordability of this model.

Marketing

In the network school and consortium school model, many families will not experience significant change as their parish school becomes part of a network of schools. Parishes may continue to designate funds to support children who attend a network school, and pastors may designate scholarships for students from their parish who attend a network school. The principal marketing points for the network model are neighborhood schools, controlled costs, and effective and efficient management of the schools. The involvement of priests in the schools to assist with religious formation and pastoral needs can also be a point to emphasize in a marketing plan.

Corporate Partnerships: Cristo Rey Network Schools

Contact Information to Learn More

www.cristoreynetwork.org

Brief History

The *Cristo Rey* schools are a unique type of network school in that all the *Cristo Rey* schools educate students at the secondary level and the network is national rather than local. The first *Cristo Rey* (Christ the King) high school opened in 1996 in Chicago. Begun by Fr. John Foley of the Society of Jesus, the *Cristo Rey* model has seen tremendous growth and has evolved into a national network of schools operated by many different religious orders, archdioceses, and dioceses. The national office of the *Cristo Rey* network provides support for local Catholic educators who want to explore starting up a new *Cristo Rey* model school in their city. Corporate partners have included the Bill and Melinda Gates Foundation and the Walton Family Foundation.

Program Description

Cristo Rey is a unique model of schooling in which schools and students partner with local businesses and corporations. Students in the schools work one day a week in local businesses or corporations, and their salary helps to offset the cost of their education.

Students gain valuable work and life experiences through their corporate internships. The schools engage in fund-raising and work with families in order to fully fund operations and education expenses.

Marketing

Local educators can convince businesses and corporations to become involved with a *Cristo Rey* school by emphasizing that students will be racially and ethnically diverse and will be taught human relations and professional work skills at the school. Students in *Cristo Rey* schools are seeking to improve their lives through hard work and education, so there is a natural appeal for this model with business, corporate, and foundation leaders. For families and students, marketing points include affordability, experience working in a business or corporate setting, faith formation in a Catholic school, and a college prep curriculum.

Further Development of the Model

To reduce dependence on fund-raising and keep school costs affordable for families, educators could consider how to expand the salary each student receives from their corporate employer. Possibilities would include working two days a week or entering into an apprenticeship agreement in which a student would work at a business or corporation during the school year and over the summer while also making a promise to return to the company after graduation from a college program. The college program could be tailored to meet the needs of both the student and the employer with the employer paying for part or all of the student's college expenses.

Corporate Partnerships: Big Shoulders Fund

Contact Information to Learn More

www.bigshouldersfund.org

Brief History

Big Shoulders began as a new source of revenue for schools in 1986 when leaders of the Catholic Church in Chicago partnered with business and civic leaders in the city. The goal of the partnership was to support access to quality elementary and secondary Catholic schools for inner city Chicago children and youth. All the parties in the partnership were convinced that access to quality Catholic schools would result in stable neighborhoods and good quality of life for the graduates of the schools.

Program Description

Big Shoulders raises funds and uses those funds to support Catholic elementary and secondary schools in the Chicago area. Big Shoulders provides operating grants, funds for staff professional development, and student scholarships. Big Shoulders also provides a way for benefactors to have hands-on involvement with schools through sharing their time and talent to assist with and improve school operations.

In 2017, Big Shoulders was approved as a scholarship granting organization or SGO by the State of Illinois. As an SGO, Big Shoulders is approved to receive corporate and benefactor donations that are then given to eligible students to use for tuition at Catholic schools in the Chicago area. The corporations and benefactors who make the donations qualify for a State of Illinois tax credit under an Illinois statute.

Marketing

Big Shoulders recruits business leaders, civic leaders, and benefactors through data-based storytelling. Big Shoulders tracks and reports high school and college enrollment rates, high school graduation rates, rates of completing a bachelor's degree, and alumni civic engagement. Big Shoulders then tells their story by comparing the outcomes of their graduates to the outcomes of graduates from other schools using the tracking data they have collected. The Big Shoulders partnership model could be replicated in other cities utilizing similar networking and marketing strategies. As more states approve scholarship tax credits, and as more scholarship granting organizations (SGOs) are created within states, the Big Shoulders school revenue model could be a natural way to leverage state tax credits and SGOs for maximum impact in Catholic schools.

Conclusion

Each of the new school models presented in this chapter has already been implemented by Catholic schools across the United States. There is ample evidence that the models presented in this chapter have been successful. I have provided contact information for each model so that you can learn more about any of the models of interest to you and so that you can also evaluate the success of a specific model for yourself. In the next chapter, we will explore best practices in accessing state and federal funds for students attending private schools as an additional way to make Catholic schools affordable.

In Chapter Seven, you will find a template to assist you with implementing new strategies to address affordability at your school. You can use the template in Chapter Seven with your school leadership team to plan out steps to make your Catholic school affordable for all families and youth who want to attend your school.

CHAPTER THREE: Broadly Supported Schools

NSBECS Benchmarks for Affordable Catholic Schools

10.3 Financial plans define revenue sources that include but are not limited to ***tuition, tuition assistance/scholarships***, endowment funds, local and regional partnerships, ***public funding***, regional cost sharing, (arch)diocesan and/or religious communities' assistance, foundation gifts, entrepreneurial options and other sources not listed.

See ***www.catholicschoolstandards.org*** for more information.

In this chapter, I share additional strategies to improve the affordability of Catholic schools. By increasing educator knowledge and skills in accessing state and federal funds for students in private schools, and by expanding parental choice in education, we can once again make Catholic schools affordable and accessible for all the students who wish to attend a Catholic school. As we slay the last vestiges of anti-Catholicism at the state and federal levels of government through concerted advocacy, broad support for private schools will finally be possible if we can make the case to the nation that Catholic schools provide an excellent return on the nation's investment.

In the two sections of this chapter that follow, I provide information and resources you can use to establish broader support for your Catholic school. But first it is important to note that from time to time, concerns are voiced in the Catholic community about the effects on Catholic schools of accepting state and federal resources. However, I do not share these concerns, so long as state and federal resources continue to flow to religious schools based on the child benefit concept and based on the principle that parents have the right to choose the education for their children.

Based on the child benefit concept, local, state, and federal resources are made available to students in private schools because giving all students access to basic resources benefits the child, and eventually will benefit the common good when the well-educated child is able to be a productive and informed citizen in the community. Providing a textbook on United States history or school transportation services to all school-age youth in a geographic region supports the common good and does not require any level of government to engage in the inner workings of a private school. These types of resources and many others have been shared with students in private schools for decades with no effect on the religious mission of Catholic schools.

Funding of private school tuition using funds generated from public taxes is a newer means of providing broader stakeholder support for Catholic schools. Whether the mechanism of support be in the form of tax credits, tax deductions, tuition vouchers, or educational savings accounts, there is no question that funding of private school tuition with local, state, and federal dollars goes beyond the types of resource sharing common in every state. But the common good is still served if all students receive a high-quality education. Also, by relying on the Supreme Court decision in *Pierce v. Society of Sisters* (268 US 510, 1925), if the funding is provided to parents who then choose the best school for their children, the government's role ends when the funds are provided to the parents to be used for the education of their children in a school that meets the government's legitimate interest that youth be educated for citizenship and employment. I would argue that tax-based funding models in which funds are given to parents can be developed in such a way that there would be no effect on the religious practice or mission of Catholic schools.

Based on the positive outcomes for Catholic schools of the funding models we have been discussing, we can confidently explore a variety of options for broad support of Catholic schools. First, we will explore options for state level support of students attending Catholic schools, and then we will explore options for federal level support of students attending Catholic schools.

Accessing State Funds & Programs for Students in Catholic Schools

Contact Information to Learn More

*American Federation for Children
https://www.federationforchildren.org/

*Children's Scholarship Fund
https://scholarshipfund.org

*EdChoice
https://www.edchoice.org/

*National Catholic Educational Association—Public policy information
www.ncea.org

*Your state Catholic conference or (arch)diocesan office

Brief History

As I documented in Chapter One of this book, the Blaine Amendments to many state constitutions came about due to anti-Catholic and anti-immigrant sentiments among large segments of the U.S. population in the 1800s and early 1900s. Additional advocacy with legislators and future court cases will likely be effective in striking down these amendments as unconstitutional (McDonald, 2020; Peterson, 2020). Two decisions by the United States Supreme Court have already put in place legal precedents that will likely provide the foundation for dismantling Blaine Amendments in state constitutions (*Espinoza v. Montana Department of Revenue*, 591 US, 2020; *Trinity Lutheran Church of Columbia, Inc. v. Comer*, 582 US, 2017).

At the same time, other factors have moved parental choice in education forward despite the limitations imposed by Blaine Amendments in some state constitutions. Parental and community dissatisfaction with some local school districts, advocacy for parental choice in the education of their children, and recognition by community stakeholders of the need to provide educational resources to all students has led to the creation of programs in various states that provide assistance for students and educators in private schools.

Program Descriptions

Each state has unique programs providing different types of assistance to private school students and educators and to parents who enroll their children in private schools. I suggest that contacting your state Catholic conference or (arch)diocesan office is the best way to begin to learn what programs and resources are available in your state. Additionally, in the next section, I provide examples of resources that are available in some states to assist with private school education. You can use these examples to learn about the types of resources that are or could be available in your state to support the education of children and youth in private schools.

Examples of State Programs

The first example of how some states are assisting students and parents with private school education is based on the principle that parents have the right to choose their children's education. In states that have passed tax legislation to assist with the education of children, parents who incur costs for the education of their children, including payment of tuition, are eligible for a state tax credit or state tax deduction. If your state has not yet passed these types of tax legislation, you can work with your state Catholic conference, (arch)diocesan office, and your school stakeholders to advocate for new legislation based on what has been successful in other states.

A second example of how some states are already assisting with the costs of private school education also involves tax legislation. In states in which scholarship tax credit legislation has been passed, interested parties can set up a scholarship granting organization or SGO. Once the SGO is established, then corporations, businesses, and individuals may donate money to the SGO and receive a state scholarship tax credit. The SGO uses the donated funds to provide scholarships to students for school tuition.

The third example of how states assist students in private schools is based on the child benefit concept. The child benefit concept holds that some resources provided to students do not directly support the religious purpose of a school while supporting the necessary education of all the students in the state. Examples of resources that some states share with students in private schools through application of the child benefit concept are textbooks, supplemental instructional services, and transportation services (McDonald, 2020).

Some states also provide tuition vouchers and educational savings accounts to parents so that parents can choose the best school for their children. The amount of the voucher differs significantly between states and is closely defined by law, policy, and practice. Parents may use the voucher or educational savings account to pay for their children's tuition at a private school. Funds from educational savings accounts can also be used for other education-related expenses.

Expansion of Programs

Advocacy with state legislators and your governor is one way to expand state support for private schools and school choice options in your state. Catholic educators and interested stakeholders, including parents and their children, need to develop the knowledge, skills, and experience necessary to engage in effective democratic advocacy.

Perhaps advocacy for parental choice in education seems like a bit of a stretch for you. But keep in mind that educators have been engaging in advocacy for many years, and programs that support private school education are growing rapidly in many different states (Table 3.1). Take the first step and talk with a representative at your state Catholic conference or (arch)diocesan office to learn how to engage in the same types of advocacy that have already proven successful for other Catholic educators.

Table 3.1 Examples of State Programs that Provide Assistance for Children & Parents Who Choose Private Schools

Number of States with Program[a]	Program Type	Explanation of Program
19	Scholarship Tax Credit	When an individual, business, or corporation donates to a private non-profit scholarship granting organization, the individual, business, or corporation receives a tax credit. The scholarship granting organization then uses the funds donated to provide scholarships for students who apply.
18	Voucher	When a parent chooses to enroll his or her child in a private school, the local school district provides the parent with an amount of money to pay for part or all the child's tuition at a private school.
08	Individual Tax Credit/ Deduction	Parents may receive state tax credits or tax deductions for the expenses related to the education of their children.
07	Education Savings Account	A parent may choose to withdraw his or her child from a public school to attend a private school. An amount of money will be deposited in a state-authorized account for the parent to use for the education of the child. This money can be used for private school tuition and fees and for other approved education-related costs.

Notes. Source for this table was edchoice.org, *School Choice in America Dashboard, updated February 2020*.
[a]Number includes the District of Columbia and Puerto Rico.

For example, advocacy can be as simple as asking legislators to visit your school and meet your students. You could also ask a legislator to attend a school event, sit on the stage, and give a short welcome or lead the pledge of allegiance. Legislators who know your students are more likely to consider the needs of your students when they consider how they will vote on school funding bills and parental choice legislation.

Creating parent networks for school choice advocacy can maximize the number of times a legislator is contacted about an issue or legislative bill. If a parent is chosen to lead the network, this leader can focus on developing a relationship with legislators so that the voices of all the parents in the network are heard more clearly.

Enlisting local union members and their organizations in advocacy is an additional step to consider. Firefighters, police officers, members of trade unions, and members of professional unions likely send their children to your school. Their unions may be able to help advocate for your school and your students with state legislators by making the argument that Catholic schools contribute to the common good and to the well-being of your state through education that propels students upwards to success.

On an even broader scale, it is also important to develop partnerships with a variety of people and organizations related to private schools. Linking families, educators, clergy, and supporters of Catholic schools with families and educators who support other private schools as well as national organizations dedicated to advancing the interests of private school education can create a larger group of voices to lobby legislators for support of private education. The American Federation for Children is one national organization seeking to advance access to private school education for all students. EdChoice is another national organization advocating for parental choice in education. The Children's Scholarship Fund is a national organization committed to assisting local stakeholders with setting up SGOs. Contact information for all of these organizations is provided in a table at the beginning of this section.

Accessing Federal Funds & Programs for Students in Catholic Schools

Contact Information to Learn More

*Catapult Learning
https://catapultlearning.com/

*Equitable Services MDEC
https://equitableservicesmdec.com/

*FACTS Education Solutions
https://factsmgt.com/facts-ed/

*National Catholic Educational Association–Public policy information
www.ncea.org

*US Department of Education–Office of Non-Public Education
https://www2.ed.gov

Brief History

In addition to state funds that support parents and children who choose private schools, the federal government provides assistance to teachers and students in private schools. The bulk of federal funds for PK-12 schools were originally authorized in the Elementary and Secondary Education Act of 1965, promoted and signed by President Lyndon Johnson. The most recent version of this legislation is the Every Student Succeeds Act

(ESSA) which was passed into law in 2015. This legislation will periodically be reviewed by Congress and renamed.

Program Descriptions

The goal of federal funding for PK-12 education is to ensure that every student is well prepared for their post-high school endeavors, whether that be immediate employment, military service, or additional education to prepare for eventual employment and active participation in society. Federal funding is especially targeted to support the success of children of low-income parents and guardians, students below grade level, and children with special learning needs.

Federal funds are not usually given directly to private schools. Following the child benefit concept, federal funds are provided for the benefit of the student, which ultimately accrues as a benefit to the nation. Instructional materials, specific types of professional development, and instructional assistance for students in private schools are paid for by a local education agency or LEA, often a tax-supported local school district. The LEA receives the federal funds and then private school officials work with LEA staff to identify which student and teacher-related expenses can be paid for by federal funds in each funding cycle. Examples of private school student and teacher expenses that may be covered by federal funds are described in Table 3.2. Additional expenses can also be eligible to be covered by federal funds through the free and reduced lunch program and the e-rate program.

Table 3.2 Examples of Private School Expenses Eligible to be Covered by Federal Funds

Title Number[a]	Program Name	Examples of Covered Expenses
Title I[b]	Improving the Academic Achievement of the Disadvantaged	• Supports for blended learning • Supplemental instructional supports • Tutoring
Title II	Preparing, Training, and Recruiting High-Quality Teachers, Principals, or Other School Leaders	• Professional development for principals, leaders, and teachers • Targeted recruitment of math and science teachers
Title III	Language Instruction for English Learners and Immigrant Students	• Development and support of programs for English language learners
Title IV	21st Century Schools	• Drug and violence prevention programs • Faculty training in trauma-informed instruction • Student counseling services • Afterschool and summer programs • Support for AP classes in STEM

[a]Title programs may be divided into smaller programs with a unique focus; for example, Title I-A and Title I-B.
[b]Title I funding is based on where students live, while Title II, III, and IV funding is based on the location of the school. Therefore, a private school representative may have to work with more than one LEA to obtain Title I funds if students at the private school reside in more than one LEA attendance area.

Accessing Funds

A wide variety of educational services, such as teacher professional development and resources for special needs students, are available to the students and staff in your school through federal government programs like the ones described in Table 3.2. But you cannot access these significant resources without a plan.

To develop a plan to access federal education resources, you first need a skilled person on your staff to oversee the process of obtaining support services that will enhance the success of students in your school. The person you designate at your school or in your school system to be responsible for obtaining and managing federal resources will need preparation to be successful. See Table 3.3 for ideas on how a principal, assistant principal, curriculum coordinator, or student services coordinator would obtain the knowledge and experience needed to effectively access federal funds for private school students and staff. See Table 3.4 for an overview of how a trained person in your school or school system would work with a local education agency or LEA to obtain resources and support for your students.

If you decide to request that a third-party provider, such as FACTS Education Solutions or Catapult Learning, assist you with managing federal funds, then the third-party provider can share best practices with the point person at your school or school system office. The fees to cover the work done on behalf of your students by a third-party provider may be covered in full or in part by federal funds, so this is a good option to consider if you do not currently have the capacity to manage federally funded support services for your students.

Table 3.3 Examples of How a Person Would Prepare to be a Student Services Coordinator

Strategy	Details
Seek Out a Mentor	Network with your Catholic schools office and with your state Catholic conference to identify individuals who have been successful in working with local education agencies (LEAs) to obtain support services for students in Catholic schools. Ask one of these persons to mentor you or a member of your staff.
Review Websites	State education agencies (SEAs) publish information about state and federal funds available to students in private schools on their websites. Your local education agency or LEA, often a school district, may also publish similar information on their website. Look for information about title funds and student support services.
Contact the National Catholic Educational Association	NCEA's Vice President of Public Policy can put you in touch with resources and assistance. Professional development meetings and webinars, sponsored by NCEA, include presentations on accessing state and federal resources.
Engage with State-Level Staff	Each state has a person designated to facilitate equitable services in public and private schools. This person will have a title akin to ombudsman or non-public school student services coordinator. Contacting this person and intentionally developing a good working relationship can be a helpful way to learn about the SEA and LEA process of allocating resources for students in PK-12 schools.

Table 3.4 Overview of the Process to Obtain Federal Education Resources

Step	Activity	Examples
1	**Collect Student Data**	**Title I:** Determine the number of students in your school or system eligible for free or reduced lunch using the same method as your local education authority (LEA). **Titles II & IV:** Collect student enrollment data on the official count day designated by your LEA. **Title III:** Determine the number of students in your school or system who meet your LEA's definition of an English language learner.
2	**Analyze & Prepare Student Data**	Check with your LEA, NCEA, or third-party provider on how to present your data.
3	**Review Local Education Authority (LEA) and State Education Authority (SEA) Guidance Documents**	Ask for copies of these documents and review them. Copies may also be available on LEA and SEA websites.
4	**Determine which Students Qualify for Services**	Identify students who are below grade level in proficiency or at risk of dropping below grade level.
5	**Engage in Consultation with Your Local Education Agency (LEA)**	Meet with the LEA title coordinator to share the student data collected and how this data supports the allocation of resources to students in the private school or system.
6	**Follow Up on the Consultation**	Send an e-mail to your LEA title coordinator summarizing the decisions you collaboratively made during your meeting. If you are not satisfied with the outcome of your meeting, contact your state education agency or the U.S. Department of Education.
7	**Report on Funds Allocated**	Contact your LEA to obtain the documents needed to describe the ways support services were used and to document the improvement of student learning outcomes.

Conclusion

In closing, I want to share with you a story concerning innovation that I read about in a book by Mark Sanborn. Some years ago, a large car manufacturer wanted to develop plans for a new car that would meet specific gas mileage criteria as well as style and size criteria. After many months of painstaking work, the manufacturer's engineers reported that the desired goal was impossible to achieve. Sometime later, when a new group of engineers looked at the plans again, they were able to meet the goal, and the car was eventually produced.

This story demonstrates that preconceptions can make it difficult to implement new ideas and strategies. My advice to you is to try some of the new strategies in this chapter to enhance the affordability and accessibility of your school for your students. If you need help, I have provided contact information for numerous organizations who have staff ready and willing to help you innovate.

In this chapter, we reviewed specific strategies you could adopt to access local, state, and federal funds to assist your students, your parents, and your educational staff. Creating broader support structures for Catholic schools moving forward will be key to their ongoing success. One way to develop this broader support is to become savvy in accessing funds already available to those who know how to ask.

In Chapter Seven, you will find a template to assist you with implementing strategies to access new funds for your school and your parents. You can use the template in Chapter Seven with your school leadership team to plan out steps to make your Catholic school more affordable and more accessible for all families and youth who want to attend your school.

Notes

CHAPTER FOUR:
Networked Schools

NSBECS Benchmarks for Partnering with Parents & Stakeholders

4.2 The leader/leadership team and faculty **assist parents/guardians in their role as the primary educators of their children in faith.**

6.4 The leader/leadership team establishes and supports **networks of collaboration** at all levels within the school community to advance excellence.

See ***www.catholicschoolstandards.org*** for more information.

In Chapters Two and Three, I provided details about the first part of my proposal for how to write a new success story for Catholic schools by once again making Catholic schools affordable for all who want to attend these schools. In this chapter, I share the second part of my proposal for how to write a new success story for Catholic schools.

In the pages that follow, I advocate for the development of networks of collaboration among educators, parents, clergy, and other important stakeholders so that a felt need for Catholic schools on the part of stakeholders drives support of the schools. Catholics between 1800 and 1965 felt it was critical to build a system of schools that would educate their children in a safe environment focused on sharing the Catholic faith. Now we need to identify what would motivate parents to enroll their children in a Catholic school today. In other words, we need to discover new points of focus for Catholic schools based on the nexus between the unique purpose of Catholic schools and the needs of parents and families today.

Developing Networks of Collaboration with Community Members & Parents

Members of your local community and your parents can assist you with discovering new points of focus for your school that will meet the felt needs of potential parents. Creative thinking and action will be necessary to discover the PK-12 school-related interests of potential parents.

Scanning the environment is one creative action step you can take. For example, stay in touch with your (arch)diocesan main office or chancery to find out when and where new parishes will be built. Another demographic change to monitor is the movement of people into new residential areas and new apartment buildings. You can stay abreast of new building and development through media sources, realtors, builders, and local leaders.

When families begin to attend a new parish or move into new family housing, your goal will be to determine what these families are looking for in a school. Through developing networks with clergy, pastoral ministers, local realtors, and day care providers, you can begin to develop an idea of potential parents' interests in educational opportunities by engaging in informal polling.

The most important action step you can take to identify new focus points for your school is to develop multiple ways to connect with parents of school-age children. Directly asking parents about what is important to them in a school is one strategy you can utilize. If you lead a grade school or have connections with a grade school, informally poll the parents of students in the grade school about their interests in educational programs for their children, including their thoughts about high school curricula and programs. Informally poll high school parents about their interests in school programs. You can discover more broadly what is of interest to parents by informally polling your current parents about their social media conversations. For example: Do they have contact with parents of school-age children through social media who have enrolled their children in other schools? If so, what are these parents saying about local schools and school programs?

Maximize Use of Existing Schools

As new parishes are built and new family housing is planned, be smart about how to utilize existing schools. If existing schools have room to enroll more students, consider utilizing those available desks before planning the construction of a new school. Even though it is a commonly held perception that families want neighborhood schools, schools that are relatively close may be just as appealing if the schools have unique programs that are of interest to potential parents.

Schools that have developed an agreement with their LEA to provide tax-supported school transportation options will have a broader geographic feeder area. The location of your school does not have to be your number one marketing point. A school that has interesting or unusual programs in key focus areas may even appeal to parents more than less specialized schools in their own neighborhoods. Being able to offer affordable and easy access to school transportation options is critical for drawing from a wider geographic region.

Examples of New Focus Points

What parents feel like their children need today is much different than what parents of even 10 years ago thought their children most needed for their future success. Therefore, it is important to stay abreast of new educational options and ideas that have appeal for parents of school-age children. To provide you with a place to begin imagining what new focus points for your Catholic school might look like, I have provided some examples in Table 4.1.

Table 4.1 Examples of New Focus Points for Your School

Focus Point	Rationale & Resources
Extended School Day and Extended School Calendar–early start and later dismissal, increased number of school days	■ Provides time for additional programs to assist below grade level students ■ Provides time for free and reduced lunch students to have breakfast, lunch, a snack, and a late afternoon meal ■ Provides time for students to be involved in clubs, co-curriculars, outdoor education, high ability programs, and the arts ■ Obviates the need for parents to arrange for afterschool daycare and summer programs
Dual Language Curriculum–students learn in a partner language for half the school day	■ Model has proven to be popular with parents (Melley, 2019) ■ Dual language schools have seen enrollment increases (Melley, 2019) ■ Global economy and immigration increasingly require people to speak multiple languages ■ Resource: Boston College Roche Center for Catholic Education
STREAM Curriculum	■ Schools that focus on science, technology, engineering, and math (STEM) are eligible for federal title program funding ■ Third-party providers, such as Eduscape, can assist with curriculum development using federal title program funding ■ Addition of religious formation and the arts to the STEM curriculum provides a unique point of differentiation for your school ■ Resource: National Catholic Educational Association
Discipling Curriculum	■ In addition to providing worship for students, students can also engage in planning liturgies and participating in the appropriate ministries of a liturgy ■ In addition to providing opportunities for service, students can discuss the explicit relationship between service work and the teachings of Jesus ■ Resource: National Catholic Educational Association publications

Develop Networks of Collaboration with Clergy & Religious

Religious formation is a natural focus point for a Catholic school. One way to redesign the religious formation program in your school is to create a network of collaboration with bishops, priests, deacons, and members of religious communities. Invite members of the clergy and religious communities to work with you in auditing and developing an innovative new faith formation program for students. The involvement of clergy and religious in helping to design your faith formation program can be a point to share with parents to emphasize the Catholic identity of your school.

Conclusion

In this chapter, we have reviewed how to develop a collaborative network with your stakeholders to discern and develop new focus points for your school. Figures 4.1 through 4.4 are a guide for you to apply your learning and begin thinking about how you will develop new focus points for your school. A planning template is also provided in Chapter Seven to assist you with the process of developing new focus points for your school.

Following this chapter, you will move into Part Two of this book. In Part Two, Dr. Ron Fussell will assist you in discerning how to share your new focus points and tell your school's new story through hiring practices and communication strategies.

Figure 4.1 Process to Identify Focus Points for Your School

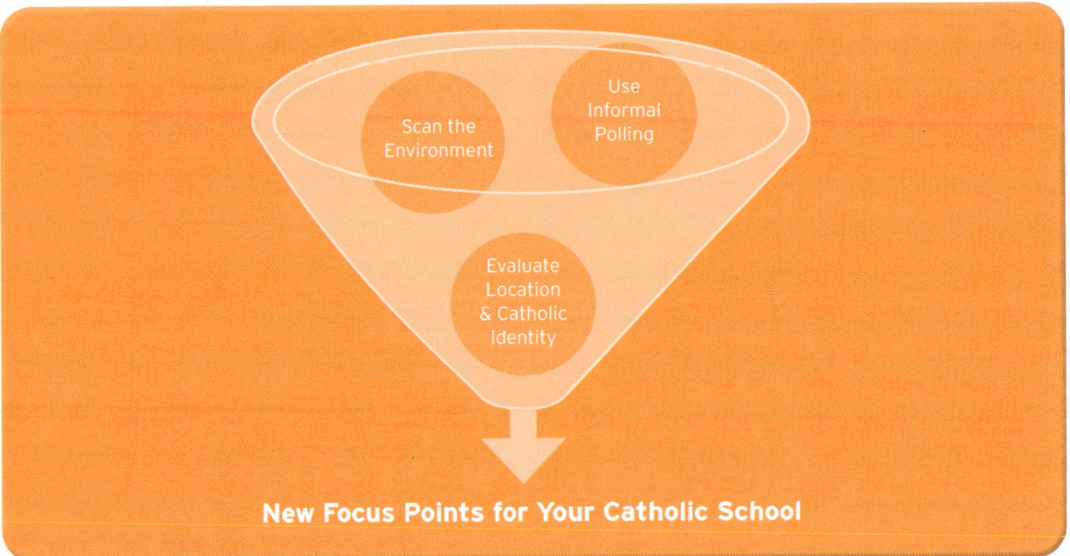

Figure 4.2 Details on Scanning & Polling

Scan Environment	Scan Environment	Use Informal Polling
Determine if new parishes are planned: check with (arch)diocese	Determine if new family housing is planned: check with builders, realtors, & leaders	Engage in informal polling in new parishes, with stakeholders, and parents

Figure 4.3 Details on Informal Polling with Parents

Current Grade School Parents

- Chat with parents in your Catholic grade school about their interests in grade school & high school programs.
- Tip: Parent and teacher conferences can be a time to meet and chat with parents.

Friends of Current Parents

- What are parents' friends saying on social media about local schools and school programs?
- Tip: Ask some parents to host gatherings online or in person and discuss this topic.

Current High School Parents

- Chat with current high school parents about their ideas for school programs.
- Tip: Parent and teacher conferences, athletic events, and fine and performing arts events provide opportunities for school leaders to chat with parents.

Figure 4.4 Details on Evaluating Location & Catholic Identity

Location	Location	Catholic Identity
Fill seats in existing schools before building a new school	Develop student transportation options to support attendance at existing schools	• Make it a hallmark of your school • Ask clergy and religious to help strengthen

Notes

PREFACE TO PART TWO

In Chapters One through Four, Fr. Simonds presented his proposal for how to write a new success story for Catholic schools. In Chapters Five and Six, I will demonstrate how to apply the principles of Fr. Simonds' proposal to hiring of faculty members and the creation of a new school communications plan.

Chapter Five

In Chapter Five, I focus on hiring of faculty because excellent faculty are your key internal storytellers. They tell your school's new story to your students and parents and create loyalty among alumni.

A focus on faculty hiring is also important if we want Catholic schools to be schools for all who want to attend. Just as Jesus welcomed all who came to him for help, the ideal Catholic school is able to advance the learning and formation of all students who want to attend. With broad local, state, and federal support as described in Chapters Two and Three, Catholic educators will be able to lead learning for students of diverse abilities and backgrounds. Hiring faculty who already have knowledge and skills in how to work with students of diverse abilities and backgrounds will be the starting point for increasing the number and diversity of students in your school.

Chapter Six

In Chapter Six, I discuss how to develop a new communications strategy because doing so will enable you to tell your story to external stakeholders. External school stakeholders are a broad group of people and organizations including corporations, benefactors, legislators, prospective parents, unions, non-profits, people in your local community, members of the clergy, and members of religious congregations. Sharing your focus points and your story with these people will enable you to develop a broad network of support for your school.

PART TWO

Telling Your School's New Story

Ronald D. Fussell, Ed.D.

CHAPTER FIVE:
Hiring Faculty to Tell Your School's New Story

NSCECS Benchmarks for Effective Faculty Hiring Practices

2.5 ***Faculty use the lenses of Scripture and the Catholic intellectual tradition in all subjects*** to help students think critically and ethically about the world around them.

2.7 The theory and practice of the ***Church's social teachings*** are essential elements of the curriculum.

3.4 Every student experiences ***role models of faith and service for social justice*** among the administrators, faculty, and staff.

4.5 Every administrator, faculty, and staff member ***visibly supports the faith life of the school community.***

11.3 Human resource policies ensure that ***competitive and just salaries, benefits***, and ***professional growth opportunities*** are provided for all staff.

See ***www.catholicschoolstandards.org*** for more information.

As the saying goes, "You can't give what you don't have." It is worth considering this wise adage when we think about the role of the Catholic school teacher. After all, Catholic school teachers have an essential role in the formation of the students entrusted to their care. A teacher in a Catholic school is not merely one who educates. Terms like "educate" and "instruct" are rarely used in Vatican documents to describe the role of the teacher. Rather, in Catholic schools, the teacher takes on a broader role in *forming* students–mind, body, and spirit–into the human beings that God intended them to be (Congregation for Catholic Education, 1982). This requires teachers who are not only professionally competent but who are also engaged with their faith and intentional about modeling it for their students. If your school's story is to be grounded upon a sturdy foundation in Catholic identity, then you need outstanding faculty members who can make your school's story come alive for students. What do Catholic school teachers need to *have* in order to *give*? In this chapter, we will answer that question by examining in greater detail the specific role of the Catholic school teacher and how Catholic schools can hire and retain effective teachers who will pen the stories of their schools on the hearts of their students.

The Catholic School Teacher: One Job, Many Facets

Take a moment to consider how teachers in the United States are generally prepared to teach. If you are, or were, a teacher, you might consider your own experiences. Perhaps your reflection squares with the common reality that most undergraduate teacher preparation programs focus primarily on professional competence in the classroom. Aspiring teachers learn about advances and best practices in instruction. They gain some experience in attending to the needs of exceptional learners. Courses in developmental and educational psychology help teacher preparation students learn more about how the brain works and how students learn. Future teachers in secondary education also grow in a specific area of study, deepening their understanding of content so that they can teach it effectively in the classroom. And in nearly all cases, aspiring teachers engage in practicum experiences that provide opportunities to practice learned skills under the watchful supervision and mentorship of an experienced teacher. In short, most preparation programs are adequate in leading novice teachers to be well-prepared in their field and competent in delivering instruction in the classroom.

Professional preparation of teachers is as important in Catholic schools as it is in public schools. We know from Canon Law that instruction which is given in Catholic schools should be "at least as academically distinguished as that in the other schools of the area" (CCC 806 §2). An *academically distinguished* school requires competent teachers who are experts in their subject area and who are capable of designing, delivering, and evaluating effective instruction to students of diverse backgrounds with a variety of learning needs. This professional competence in part leads to a commitment to the academic success of *all* students who attend the school (Vatican II, 1965). Vatican documents identify the professional competence of teachers as a "necessary condition" for Catholic schools to meet their overall goal (Congregation for Catholic Education, 2014, II.7).

In a Catholic school, however, the role of the teacher extends beyond excellent instruction and also touches on the very core of what it means to *form* students within the context of a Christian community. This broader view of student formation, which is usually not addressed in teacher preparation programs, necessarily extends into matters of faith. Put simply, Catholic school teachers in *all* content areas need to be prepared not only in the latest and best instructional practices, but they also need to be prepared to integrate Catholic doctrine, principles, and culture across the curriculum and in the classroom. Moreover, Catholic school teachers must have a passion for the spiritual mission of the school and seek to inspire that same passion in their students.

When I have had the opportunity to ask teachers about what inspired them to take on a ministry in Catholic education, they usually recall encounters with teachers of previous generations who exemplified engaging in formation of the whole student. That is why I firmly believe that if you want to write a new story for your Catholic school, the teachers you hire need to be able to engage in formation of the whole student.

What does an excellent Catholic school teacher candidate look like? Put simply, an excellent Catholic school teacher candidate is one who is well-prepared to illuminate knowledge with the light of faith (Vatican II, 1965).

Recruiting and Hiring Excellent Catholic School Teachers

Seeing a comprehensive hiring process through from beginning to end involves attending to many interconnected steps that involve many different people. Too often, the steps in the hiring process occur in a vacuum, which can lead to a disjointed process that results in the wrong candidate getting the position. Therefore, I recommend developing and using a coordinated process for faculty hiring that begins with graduate outcomes and ends with targeted professional development.

Figure 5.1 A Coordinated Process for Faculty Recruitment & Hiring

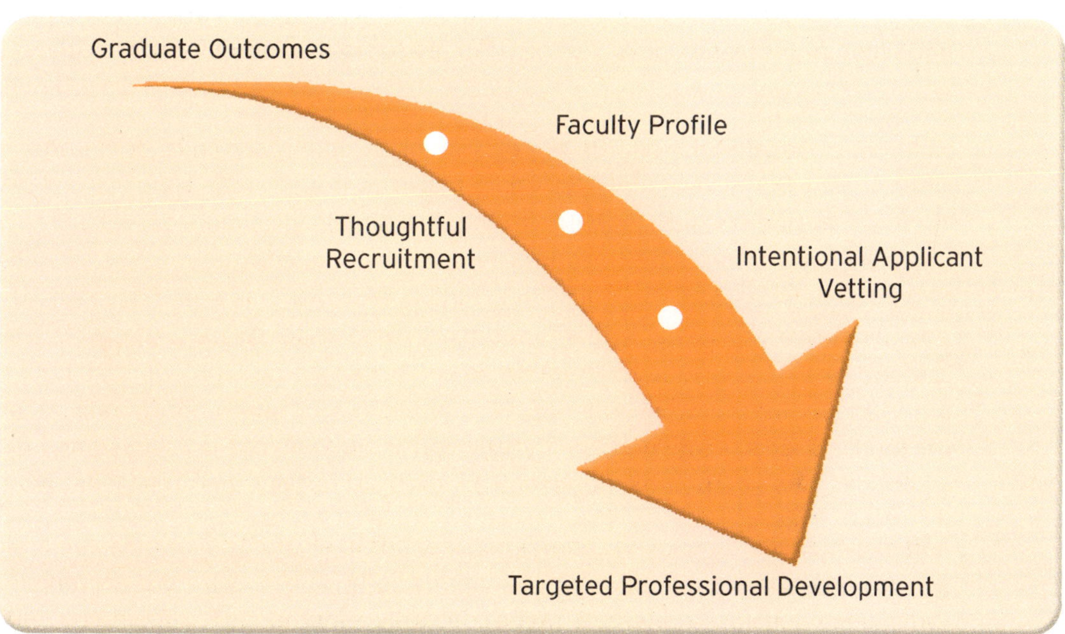

Using Graduate Outcomes in the Hiring Process

One approach to curriculum design encourages curriculum writers to begin with the end in mind. Called "backwards design," the process requires an initial understanding of the enduring outcomes hoped for at the completion of a unit of instruction. You and your leadership team can use this same backwards design model for recruitment and hiring of faculty. In Catholic schools, the ultimate programmatic outcomes can take the form of a profile of what you hope to see in students when they leave your school and move on to the next phase of their lives. These profiles are sometimes called "graduate profiles" or "grad at grad" statements. Regardless of what they are called, profiles are collaboratively developed, written down, and embraced by all within the school community. With a common understanding of what you and your team hope to see in students when they leave the school, your school team will be in a better position to hire teachers who have the knowledge, skills, and behaviors necessary to bring those hopes to fruition.

Graduate profiles are not merely aspirational statements about your hopes for your graduates. Rather, these statements reflect a *shared commitment* among all those who have a role in forming students. The key word here is *commitment*, which comes from the Latin word *committere*, meaning to "to unite, connect, combine; to bring together" (*Online Etymology Dictionary*, n.d.). You and your team can use the following set of questions to inspire collaboration and guide the development and review of a graduate profile:

1. In what ways do we hope our students will change during their years at our school?
2. In what ways will our graduates be recognizable as disciples of Jesus when they leave our school?
3. What hopes do we have for our graduates in terms of married life, priesthood, religious life, and ministerial roles in parishes?
4. What hopes do we have for our graduates in terms of their pursuit of happiness?
5. What are the key focus points that set our graduates apart from all others; for example, dual language competency, STEM competency, prepared to be active disciples, prepared to excel in the arts.

Developing a Faculty Profile Statement to Use in the Hiring Process

If your school has a well-developed graduate profile, it makes it possible to phrase expectations for teachers in more concrete terms. This is because you can connect what you hope for your students with what you expect from your teachers. A well-developed faculty profile will answer the question: *What knowledge, skills, experiences, and ways of living would characterize a faculty member who would be able to prepare our students to actualize our vision for graduates*. Consider the example in Table 5.1, which demonstrates how a faculty profile statement could be aligned with components of a graduate profile.

Table 5.1 Example of Aligning Graduate Outcomes with a Faculty Profile

Dimensions of a Graduate at Graduation[a]	Profile of a Faculty Member: Preparation in the Field[b]
Graduates Will Be Open to Growth	A teacher at X school should understand the developmental needs of the students whom he or she will be teaching, demonstrated by coursework, professional development, and professional experience.
Graduates Will Be Intellectually Competent	A teacher at X school should demonstrate competence in his or her field and in effective pedagogy, as demonstrated by coursework, professional development, and experience.
Graduates Will Be Religious	A teacher at X school should demonstrate an understanding of how Catholic doctrine and Catholic social teaching align with his or her subject area.
Dimensions of a Graduate at Graduation	**Profile of a Faculty Member: Experience in Co-curricular Areas**
Graduates Will Be Religious	A teacher at X school should be active in his or her faith, as evidenced through engagement in parish life and/or faith-based organizations and should demonstrate an interest in and involvement with student faith-based organizations.
Graduates Will Be Loving	A teacher at X school should have experience with and a desire to form healthy and appropriate relationships with students outside the classroom that respect the mystery of the other person.
Graduates Will Be Committed to Doing Social Justice	A teacher at X school should have experience engaging in service that responds to the needs of the most marginalized, and he or she should inspire students to do the same through participation in school, faith and service programs.

[a]The dimensions of a Jesuit school graduate at graduation are based on the document *Go Forth & Teach: The Characteristics of Jesuit Education*. [b]Additional dimensions of a faculty profile could include experience in the field, teaching experience, experience forming others as disciples of Jesus, examples of living as a disciple of Jesus, and experiences of serving diverse students.

Developing a faculty profile can and should be a collaborative process. The school community will more likely embrace a faculty profile that is collaboratively developed. Below is a list of possible strategies you can use to develop your faculty profile statement that will be aligned with your profile of graduates at graduation.

- A principal could set aside time during monthly faculty meetings to address one dimension of a graduate profile statement, asking the question: *What skills, experiences, and values do faculty members need to prepare students for graduation on dimension X?*

- Using online collaboration tools such as Google Docs, small groups of teachers could collaborate asynchronously to fill in or suggest revisions to a faculty profile document like the one in Table 5.1. A steering committee comprised of administrators and teachers could then synthesize those contributions into a single document.
- Teachers could collaborate in small groups during a spiritual retreat to discuss how the day-to-day work of teachers in the school intersects with the spiritual dimensions of a graduate profile statement. A group recorder could share notes with a steering committee. The steering committee, comprised of administrators and teachers, could then synthesize all of the small group contributions into statements to be included in a faculty profile.

Thoughtful Recruitment of Teacher Candidates

Consider for a moment the process that your Catholic school uses to recruit teachers.

- From where does your school recruit new teachers?

The answer to the question I have posed will reveal important information about the emphasis that your school places on hiring the best storytellers for your Catholic school. Of course, Catholic schools can and should post open positions to the usual job boards that attract teacher candidates from a variety of backgrounds. However, it can be even more helpful to engage in thoughtful recruiting efforts that are likelier to draw candidates who prioritize the spiritual dimension of education. Posting open positions on your diocesan Catholic school website, or on the National Catholic Educational Association career center, can draw candidates who are predisposed to the unique ministry of being a Catholic school teacher.

Another way to attract excellent Catholic school teacher candidates is to build a relationship with a Catholic college or university that has an established teacher preparation program. If that institution's program specializes in Catholic education, even better! It is not uncommon that student teachers from Catholic colleges who complete their final field placement in a PK-12 Catholic school will go on to become thriving professionals in that school community.

Additionally, there are many Catholic colleges and universities that offer service-through-teaching programs that place aspiring educators in Catholic schools, pay them a stipend, and partner with the school for their ongoing formation. For a complete list of institutions with service-through-teaching programs, you can visit the University Consortium for Catholic Education website (*ucceconnect.com*). These service-through-teaching programs are often regional in nature and there may be a program near you seeking a partnership with a school like yours. Aspiring Catholic school teachers who complete these programs are committed to Catholic education, are prepared to tell the story of the schools in which they work, and typically remain in their schools for many years after completing their teacher education program.

You may also find it helpful to develop programming to form and develop teachers right in your own school. This would require staying connected with graduates after they graduate from the PK-12 system and enter into professional life. In my time as a Catholic school administrator, I have come to understand that the career path of an effective Catholic school teacher is not always through a traditional teacher preparation program. By engaging with alumni who are predisposed to match the personal qualities and values present in your faculty profile, you can encourage those graduates to continue to discern a ministry in Catholic education. Many states have alternative teacher certification programs, often in critical need areas, and these programs can be useful for teachers who are best served by a non-traditional preparation program. These days, it is possible to bring in new teachers with rich backgrounds in their field who are willing to grow and develop the necessary pedagogical skills while working in your school.

Catholic schools in the United States were built in large part by women and men religious whose selfless sacrifices led to the establishment of a thriving system of local and regional Catholic schools. Today, members of the clergy and members of religious communities can still play an important role in your Catholic school. The following strategies can help you and your leadership team recruit these important members of our faith community to work in your school.

- Contact your Catholic schools office, diocesan chancellor, or vicar for clergy and express your interest in placing a priest in your school as a teacher.
- Correspond with a local seminary that prepares aspiring priests to express your interest in welcoming a seminarian to your school community for a pastoral field placement experience.
- Contact provincials and/or education directors of religious orders that specialize in educational ministries to inquire about the possibility of a sister, brother, or religious priest teaching in your school.

A Note about Compensation

It is no secret that Catholic schools have typically been unable to offer salary and benefits packages that are comparable to what teachers receive in public schools. However, I think it is important to mention that lowering salaries to meet financial objectives is counterproductive. If your school lowers salaries, teachers will not stay at your school and you will lose some of your best storytellers! Market salaries, or as close as you can get to market salaries, are required to recruit and retain the best teachers.

When recruiting teachers for your school, it is important to present a comprehensive picture of the benefits of working in a Catholic school. Of course, discussing retirement plans, health care options, and other tangible benefits is important. However, there are other important dimensions to discuss as well. For example, tuition remission benefits can entice teachers to sign on at your school if they have or plan to have children who will attend a Catholic school. In some areas in the United States, tuition remission benefits and tuition discounting extend to local Catholic colleges and universities. The intangible benefit of working in a faith community is also important to mention. A school community that takes seriously the Catholic ethos and encourages teachers to connect their personal faith lives to the work that they do with their students can be very attractive to committed Catholics.

Intentional Applicant Vetting

In my experience as a Catholic school leader and scholar, I have had the opportunity to build relationships with many Catholic school educators. At one school I know about, there was an institutional legend about the hiring of a teacher who really struggled in the school community. As the story goes, when hiring for the open position, the school principal asked the secretary to stack the resumes of the applicants from best to worst. However, the secretary stacked them from worst to best. The principal selected the worst resume off the top of the stack, invited that applicant in for an interview, and hired him on the spot. That teacher was not an effective storyteller, but because the school's teacher supervision process was also not effective, that teacher made a career of derailing school improvement efforts and sabotaging the hard work of others. What a great example of how not to recruit, hire, and retain Catholic school teachers!

The anecdote that I shared about the troublesome teacher speaks to the importance of a structured process that seeks to determine *fit*. And when it comes to hiring, it is all about fit—for the school and for the applicant. Setting up an interview team or search committee will enable you to find the person who is the right fit for your school, share the workload involved in hiring, and also enable you to gain insights into candidates that you might otherwise miss.

I recommend you select members for the interview team who are veteran faculty and match your school's profile of an excellent teacher. Each member of the interview team will begin the process by reviewing candidate applications. You may want to have one or two people do an initial review of applications to eliminate any applications that do not meet basic criteria necessary for the position.

In Table 5.2, I provide some suggestions about how to review each piece of an application for a teaching position. It is critical to review each candidate's application carefully and collaboratively because if you misplace your priorities in the vetting process, you might end up with a teacher who will be unhappy at your school and unable to effectively tell your school's story.

Table 5.2 Evaluating Components of a Catholic School Teacher Employment Application

Application Component	Questions to Consider
Cover Letter	1. How does the applicant provide context for what is in the resume? 2. Does the applicant identify anything that he or she is passionate about? If so, how does their passion relate to your faculty profile and what you are looking for in this teaching position?
Resume	1. Does the candidate have specific preparation in Catholic education? 2. Does the candidate have specific experience working in a Catholic school? If not, what would lead you to believe that he or she might be an effective storyteller for your school? 3. Are there any unexplained gaps in work experience in the resume? 4. Are the references current, and can they speak to the candidate's potential fit in a Catholic school like yours?
Transcripts	1. Does the candidate's coursework indicate requisite preparation in the content area? 2. Does the candidate's coursework indicate that they will be able to approach their subject through a lens of Catholic identity?
Reference Letters	1. Do the reference letters confirm the passions, strengths, and interests that the applicant states elsewhere in the application? 2. Do the reference letters contain any obscure or vague language that may suggest that the candidate might not be a good fit for your school?

As your interview team begins to choose candidates who show potential for telling your school's story, your team will eventually bring the most promising candidates in for a series of interviews. Work with your hiring team to decide how many interviews will be conducted for each candidate. Also discuss with your team the important dimensions of a professional interview. In Table 5.3, I have provided some key dimensions that ought to be included in every interview process.

Table 5.3 Dimensions of an Effective Interview Process

Dimension	Description
Consistency	Your interview process should be *consistent* from candidate to candidate to ensure that each applicant has a fair chance to tell his or her story. If you are not consistent in how you ask questions, you will not be able to evaluate a group of candidates objectively.
Alignment	Your interview questions should be *aligned* to your faculty profile, ensuring that the interview yields the information you need to make the hiring decision.
Collaboration	Your interview process should be *collaborative*, engaging others in the design of the interview questions and in conducting the actual interviews.
Relevancy	The interview questions should ask candidates to draw upon *relevant* experiences in their personal and professional preparation, confirming their talents, strengths, and passions presented in their applications.

As noted in Table 5.3, the best interview questions are the ones that have been developed through a collaborative process that includes administrators and teachers. Teachers play a pivotal role in the evangelizing mission of a Catholic school, and it is critical that you have a variety of people involved in the interview process so that you gain a true impression of each candidate's potential fit at your school (Cook, 2015).

Interview questions need to be thoughtfully crafted and aligned with your faculty profile in order to elicit essential information about how a candidate might be able to tell your school's story. In Table 5.4, I provide some sample interview questions aligned with some key qualities from a faculty profile. Additional topics might include questions about the candidate's situation in life (single, married, clergy, religious)[1], questions about the candidate's experiences with living the faith, questions about the candidate's experiences with forming disciples, and questions about the candidate's experiences with equity and diversity.

[1]The U.S. Supreme Court ruled in *Our Lady of Guadalupe School v. Morrissey-Berru* (591 US 2020) that the First Amendment to the United States Constitution frees church-related organizations from governmental interference or involvement in their hiring practices related to ministers and teachers given the responsibility of teaching a religious faith to students. This case indicates that teachers in Catholic schools are included under the ministerial exception principle. Schools should clearly use the language of *minister* or *teacher of the faith* in employment contracts for all teachers to ensure protection under the First Amendment for employment decisions. In addition to questions about state in life, candidate's may also be asked about their practice of the Catholic faith, including their ability to participate fully in the Sacramental life of the Catholic Church.

Table 5.4 Examples of Aligned Interview Questions

Question Topic Aligned with Criterion from a Faculty Profile	Sample Interview Questions
Preparation in the Field	Tell me about a course or professional development experience that you think has prepared you well to work in this school.
Experiences in the Field/ Experiences in the Classroom	Take me back to a time that you felt especially formed you as an educator in your field or content area. What stands out about that time?
Classroom Management Experience	Take me back to a time when you were challenged by student behaviors in the classroom. What did you learn from that experience? How does it fit with the mission of this school?
Experience with Co-curriculars	How have your experiences outside the classroom with co-curriculars shaped your relationships with students?

While being prepared for interviews with well-crafted and aligned interview questions is critical, it is just as important to develop norms to guide the conduct of the members of the interview team. In Table 5.5, I share some norms for interview teams that you can use to set expectations and ground rules for the members of your hiring team.

Table 5.5 Examples of Aligned Interview Questions

Search Committee Norm	Corresponding Scripture Quote
We will respect the dignity of all candidates both during interviews and when in private discussions.	"Put away all malice and all guile and insincerity and envy and all slander" (1 Peter 2:1).
We will prioritize listening over talking.	"Know this, my dear brothers and sisters: everyone should be quick to hear, slow to speak, slow to wrath" (James 1:19).
We will respect and honor the confidentiality of the applicants.	"That you may act discreetly, and your lips guard what you know" (Proverbs 5:2).
We will position ourselves as learners who want to know about the candidates and their experiences.	"The wise person also may hear and increase in learning" (Proverbs 1:5a).

After applications have been reviewed and the most qualified candidates have been interviewed, the search committee must discern which candidate is the best fit for the school. This final stage of the hiring process, like all of the other stages, works best when the hiring decision is both transparent and collaborative. Transparency results from defining a decision-making process prior to starting the hiring process and then using that process to make the final hiring decision. Collaboration results when the interview team has the opportunity to share their point of view on the final candidates with the person or persons who will make the final decision. If the decision-maker chooses to hire a candidate not rated as the top candidate by the interview team, then, in the spirit of transparency and collaboration, the decision-maker ought to explain the reasons for his or her choice.

Targeted Professional Development

Take a moment now and reflect on your first few months in your first Catholic school teaching position.

- How would you characterize the first few months in your first teaching position?
- Were you prepared to start telling your school's story?
- Did the school provide targeted initial professional development and faith formation based on your needs?

If you are like many teachers whom I have encountered in my travels and experiences, the answer to the three questions I posed may well be "no." That is unfortunate, because during the hiring process, the interview team learns a good deal about each candidate. The combined insights of the interview team members can be used to map out and develop professional development and faith formation for the newly hired teacher that can begin even before the first day of class (T. Uhl. personal communication. May 26, 2017). In Table 5.6, I share some guidelines you and your school team can use to craft targeted professional development and faith formation programs for your newly-hired faculty that will build seamlessly on the hiring process.

Table 5.6 Guidelines for Crafting Targeted Professional Development

Quality of Experience	Rationale
Differentiated	Strengths and growth areas of each new faculty member were documented during the hiring process, and this information will be used to create targeted professional development plans.
Encounter-based	The ideal way for new faculty to learn what it means to be an effective teacher is to talk with master teachers who can provide mentoring and tips, so each new faculty member will work with a mentor.
Year-long	New teachers are constantly having new experiences and encountering new issues, so mentors will meet with new teachers throughout their first year in the profession.
Utilize a Cohort Model	New teachers are walking the same path, so opportunities will be provided for them to gather and share their experiences as a seamless part of professional development.
Include the Faith Dimension	The Catholic school teacher engages in student faith formation, so professional development will support the ongoing faith development of each new teacher.

Conclusion

Nothing can be more supportive or more destructive of a school's culture than its faculty. Your faculty will shoulder much of the load of telling your school's story to your students. If your teachers' personal values and experiences align with your school's profile of an excellent teacher, then your faculty are more likely to be adept at telling your school's story. Therefore, the key lesson of this chapter is to align your hiring process with your faculty profile. When Catholic schools are intentional about hiring teachers who will rejoice in telling their school's story, new teachers will quickly take on the essential role of student faith formation.

As we come to the conclusion of this chapter, I want to provide a quick preview of the next chapter. In Chapter Six, I will discuss how to implement Fr. Simonds' proposal for writing a new story for Catholic schools through a communications plan, and I will focus on how to tell your story to your external stakeholders.

Before moving on to Chapter Six, however, you may find it helpful to turn to Chapter Seven. In Chapter Seven, Fr. Simonds has provided a planning template that you can use to map out an effective hiring process based on your faculty profile. This planning template can also be used to guide professional development for leaders of the initiative and for creating an accountability process for leaders.

Notes

CHAPTER SIX:

Telling Your School's New Story With a Communications Plan

NSBECS Benchmarks for an Effective Communications Plan

10.7 The governing body and leader/leadership team ***provide families access to information about tuition assistance*** and long-term planning for tuition and Catholic school expenses.

13.1 The communications/marketing plan requires school leader/leadership team and staff person(s) to ensure the implementation of ***contemporary, multiple information technologies to reach targeted audiences***, and to establish reliable and secure databases and ***accountability to stakeholders***.

See ***www.catholicschoolstandards.org*** for more information.

Take a moment to consider the state of Catholic education in the first half of the 20th century. Despite many challenges, Catholic schools flourished. Equipped with a mandate that Catholic parents ought to send their children to Catholic schools and blessed with the selfless service of the women and men religious and priests who taught and led in these schools, the Church's educational ministry quickly grew into the United States' second great school system (Walch, 2003). Catholic elementary schools during this period were a dynamic extension of parish life, fiercely protecting the cultural identity of the parish and the families who worshiped in the parish. Catholic secondary schools served as places where graduating elementary students could continue their education in an environment rich with Catholic identity, expressed through the charismatic values of the religious orders that staffed many of these schools.

Beginning with the Second Vatican Council and continuing well into the 21st century, the focus of Catholic education has shifted. Catholic schools, whose attention was previously directed towards protecting students from Protestant influences in public education, have now redirected their efforts to be places that welcome diversity as a reflection of their new evangelizing mission.

The merger of Catholic parish schools in many dioceses due to declining Mass attendance has given rise to alternative forms of governance that allow Catholic schools to reach more families, even non-Catholic families. And while enrollment statistics are still on the decline, Catholic schools that have remained open during this time serve a more diverse group of students and families. Jesus said, "Let the children come to me, and do not prevent them; for the kingdom of heaven belongs to such as these" (Matthew 19:15). The way this desire of Jesus to teach the little ones is practiced in today's Catholic schools tells a compelling story of optimism and hope for the future of the Catholic Church and Catholic education.

Clearly times have changed, but unfortunately, the way we talk about Catholic schools sometimes has not changed. This lack of change in our rhetoric is problematic given that parents and students are faced with many more options for education than in previous generations. Today's families are courted by charter schools, magnet schools, and even online schools as alternatives to public education. Public schools are savvier about marketing and advocacy as well, and enrollment is as important to them as it is to the Catholic school community. The expansion of competition in the school enrollment market amid a diminishing pool of students requires a communications strategy that engages this reality.

Years ago, it was enough for a Catholic school just to post an announcement in the parish bulletin that listed when the school's open houses would occur, and that would lead to a waiting list for prospective students. Today, enrollment management takes a coordinated effort that reaches a broader audience with appropriate messaging.

What Drives Parents to Make School Choice Decisions?

In recent years, scholars and educators have done surveys to better understand how parents make school choice decisions for their children. In a series of studies conducted by EdChoice (2017, 2018, 2019), adults revealed several key drivers that they would consider when discerning the choice of a school for their children. In the studies by EdChoice, the top reason that adults said they would choose a public school was socialization opportunities for students. Using this research finding, Catholic school communications officers can address opportunities for student socialization in their communications to enhance the appeal of Catholic schools with a new group of parents.

Survey respondents in the same studies indicated that the top reason they would choose to *homeschool* children would be safety. Once again, Catholic school communications officers can use this research finding to focus their message to parents. Addressing concerns such as bullying and sharing student perceptions of the school environment can be effective talking points with prospective parents. In Table 6.1, I share the top reasons respondents stated they would choose a private school for their children. The reasons are not presented in rank order but are instead grouped by themes.

Table 6.1 Top Reasons U.S. Adults Would Choose a Private School for Their Children (grouped by themes)

Individual attention for students
Student:Teacher ratio
Quality of education
Better teachers
Academic program quality and results
Structured environment
Religious education

Note. Information in this table is based on EdChoice (2017, 2018, 2019).

In another national study commissioned by the National Catholic Educational Association (FADICA, 2018), a broad group of parents provided qualitative and quantitative feedback that answered questions about how they make decisions about private school enrollment for their children. This study confirmed that parents are "well-informed, savvy consumers" (p. 3), but researchers also noted that parents do not always view Catholic schools as a good option for their children. The study went on to summarize that there were vast misconceptions about Catholic schools among the parents surveyed, and that "*a focus on religious instruction alone* in external communications and marketing materials will not increase enrollment in Catholic schools" (p. 4; emphasis added). The findings of the study published by FADICA are presented in Table 6.2 in rank order and echo some of the same themes from the EdChoice studies we discussed earlier. The fact that religious faith is the lowest of the nine priorities that parents look at when choosing a school for their children emphasizes the point that Catholic schools must tell a convincing story about their schools that includes religion but does not stop at the fact that religious instruction is provided.

Table 6.2 Reasons Parents Would Choose a Private School for Their Children (rank ordered)

1. Emphasizes individual and critical thinking
2. Prepares children to enter the job market successfully
3. Prepares children for college
4. Emphasizes development of communications skills
5. Engages in meaningful measuring and monitoring of student progress
6. Emphasizes moral development of students
7. Includes diversity within the school community
8. Has a sense of community
9. Emphasizes instruction in religious faith

Note. This table is based on research published by FADICA (2018).

Findings from the studies we have discussed make the point that Catholic schools must enter new relational and communications spaces to intentionally connect the school's spiritual story with all other facets of school life. It is not enough to say that your Catholic school is strong in its Catholic identity and the religious formation of students. You and your team must explain how your school's Catholic identity and spiritual mission are a catalyst that strengthens academics, critical thinking skills, preparation for post-graduation opportunities, and moral development. To tell this broader story to your external stakeholders, you need a robust communications strategy that reaches a broader audience through your school's website and social media feeds.

Getting Started with a Communications Plan

I have devised a series of questions to get you started thinking about a new communications plan for your school. Take some time now to read through each question and jot down some answers.

1. What is your school's communications strategy?
2. Does it have one?
3. If so, is it written down?
4. How does your school engage with external stakeholders in an ongoing way?

If your school is like so many others I am familiar with, you do not yet have a communications plan. There are numerous reasons why communications planning has not yet been addressed in many schools. In smaller Catholic schools, limited resources make communications planning difficult. In larger Catholic schools, the complexity of school programs and the communications process often result in gaps in what is communicated and how communication is accomplished. However, based on the research we have reviewed, schools must develop robust communications strategies. So, let's get started with developing or improving your school's communications plan.

Emphasizing Key Content on Your School Website

Notre Dame Cristo Rey High School is located in Methuen, MA. Take some time to look at the screenshot of the Notre Dame Cristo Rey website. What stands out as you look at the screenshot? (see Figure 6.1).

Figure 6.1 Screenshot of Notre Dame Cristo Rey High School's Website

Your communications strategy should emphasize key content that highlights intersections between what is important to your school and what drives parents to make decisions about school choice. The first and perhaps most obvious communications tool you can use to tell your story to external stakeholders is your school's website. In the webpage shared in Figure 6.1, one design element, the motto, stands out from all the other elements on the webpage. The text, "*Educating for Life*," connects Catholic identity themes of doctrine and social justice with parent school choice drivers such as academic preparation and career readiness. Dual colors were used to present the motto and the highlighting around the motto are eye-catching. Moreover, the carousel (the main image that constantly changes when viewed online) emphasizes the diversity of the students and other stakeholders in the school, as well as the school's innovative partnerships with local businesses, which speak to parent interests in career preparation for their children.

You can also communicate important and eye-catching information on your school's website. Take a few moments now to look at your school's website landing page (the first page that comes up when someone searches for your school). Evaluate what stands out and how those features communicate the core purpose and priorities of your school and also address the drivers of parent school choice for their children.

Emphasizing Key Content in Your Social Media Feeds

Your social media feeds can also convey important information–both stated and implied –about your school. Pause your reading now and scroll through your school's social media feeds.

- Are the postings current?
- What do the postings imply is important at your school?
- Do the social media posts tell the story about your school that you want to be told?

Now that you have reviewed some of your school's social media feeds, take a moment to review the Facebook post from Saint Thomas Aquinas High School in Dover, NH, as presented in Figure 6.2. The text and picture in this Facebook post convey several important pieces of information.

Figure 6.2 Facebook Post Example from Saint Thomas Aquinas High School

St. Thomas Aquinas High School is at
St. Thomas Aquinas High School (New Hampshire)
March 24 at 11:35 AM • Dover, NH

Integrating our Catholic identity with our athletic program is vital to our Catholic mission at St. Thomas Aquinas. Last evening, our STA athletic captains, team leaders, coaches, Athletic Director, and Director of Campus Ministry gathered to discuss ways to ensure our Catholic identity shines through our athletic program. Team prayers, service projects, special traditions were among the many discussion topics and reflections. We are so proud of our STA Athletic Program for ensuring that "Saints Pride" begins and ends with God. Saints Pride! #saintspride #stalux #luxintenebris

First, it is clear from the text that the school's successful athletics program is founded upon a commitment to the school's Catholic identity. This school is telling people how

their Catholic identity makes every aspect of the school better. Second, the image and text both indicate that community and working together are important at the school (recall that *community and developing communications skills* are attributes parents look for in a school; see Table 6.2). When asked about this post, the president of Saint Thomas Aquinas High School said, "Our vision at STA is to constantly strengthen our total curriculum on *Faith & Reason*. . . . Integrating athletics and academics is a core goal with the view that sports are integral—not separate from—the academic endeavor."

The president of STA makes a great point. The goal of a good Catholic school communications plan is not to downplay or ignore faith formation or religious education. The goal of a good communications plan is to tell your school's complete story in such a way that people who hear your story will want to hear more. You want to draw people in to take a closer look at your school, and only then will you have the opportunity to share the riches of a Catholic education with a broader group of families.

Changing Parents' Minds With Your Communications Plan

As you discern the focus points that you want to share in your online and social media communications, remember that there is a large group of parents who are not sending their children to Catholic schools. What would change their minds?

A focus on safety and bullying prevention in your messaging would be a good place to start. Recall that in the preface to Part One of this book, Fr. Simonds noted that there are virtually as many children being homeschooled in the United States as there are children in Catholic schools in the United States. For this very large group of parents who homeschool their children, school safety is a primary concern. Addressing school safety in your communications will speak to this group of parents and get their attention.

Socialization is also important for parents as they consider a school for their children. The findings from both studies discussed earlier in this chapter speak to the fact that parents desire a strong and supportive community for their children, no matter the grade level. Including information and pictures about student social experiences is important if you want to interest new parents in considering your school for their children.

Highlighting Graduation Outcomes & Parent Priorities in Your Communications Plan

Another way to sharpen your school's communications focus is to link your school's student graduation outcomes with the parent school choice priorities noted in Tables 6.1 and 6.2. You can use your online presence and social media feeds to tell the stories of students and alumni who epitomize those outcomes and parent priorities. For example, you could highlight awards that students have received and the success of co-curricular teams and programs. You could also include brief videos of students, parents, and others telling the story of your school through their positive experiences. Remember, people respond to stories and not just facts. Consider this series of tweets from Bishop Brady

High School, a diocesan high school located in Concord, NH (Figure 6.3).

Figure 6.3 Tweets from Bishop Brady High School

Bishop Brady HS @BishopBradyHS • Apr 23, 2019
Many of our students are working hard this week in West Virginia supporting Habitat for Humanity. Way to go Giants!

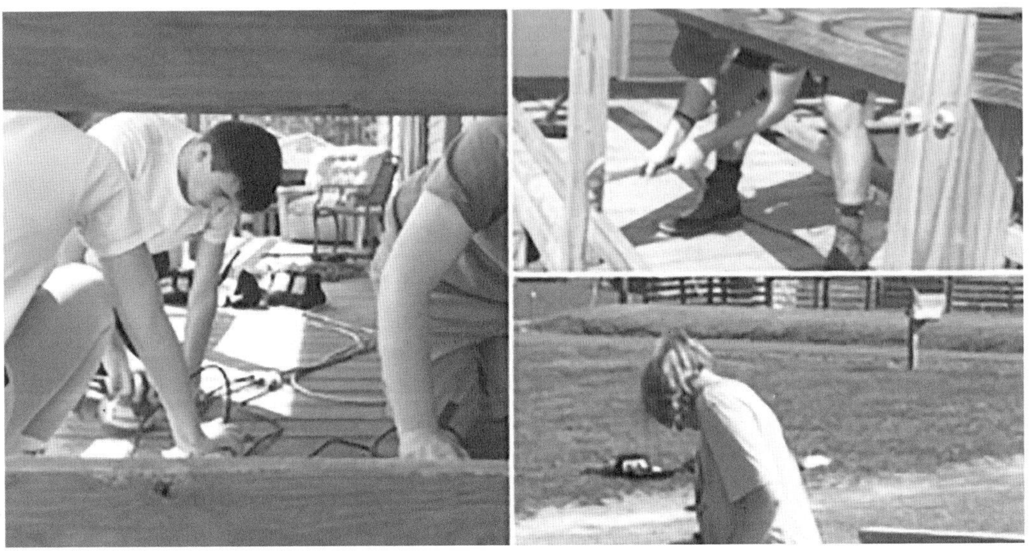

Bishop Brady HS @BishopBradyHS • Apr 30, 2019
Our Interfaith Prayer Service...

Figure 6.3 Tweets from Bishop Brady High School (continued)

Bishop Brady HS @BishopBradyHS • May 7, 2019
On May 7th, Dr. Christerson's Anatomy and Physiology students visited Concord Orthopaedics to hear from medical professionals about the many options in the health field. Many thanks to Concord Orthopaedics for their hospitality!

Tweets like these tell vivid stories of how the school's students embody certain dimensions of the school's "Vision of a Bishop Brady Graduate at Graduation" while also speaking to the priorities of parents in choosing a school for their children.

- The Habitat for Humanity tweet is an example of living as a person in service to others and relates to the parent priority on student moral development noted in Table 6.2.
- The interfaith prayer service tweet is an example of celebrating diversity found in other religions and relates to the parent priority on diversity noted in Table 6.2.
- The tweet about a class visiting an orthopedic practice is an example of intelligently exploring a variety of possibilities and relates to parent priorities for quality post-high school preparation as noted in Table 6.2.

Effectively Sharing Information on Your Website

As you think about how your school tells its story in the online forum, remember that on average, someone visiting your website will only look at it for 45 seconds (Sevell+Sevell, Inc., 2021). This speaks to the fact that people today prefer information in small, digestible units. Efficiency is essential, and people visiting your website want quick access to key information. As you work out how to tell your school's story on your website, consider developing an infographic or one-page summary that illustrates key information about your school, such as the following:

- Faculty size or faculty to student ratio
- High schools or colleges that your alumni attend
- High school graduation rate
- College acceptance rate
- College completion rate in four years or five years
- Statistics from alumni surveys about how their experiences in the school prepared them for life
- Tuition assistance programs
- Tax deductions available for school-related expenses
- Vouchers and education savings account options to cover tuition

The Xaverian Brothers High School "fast facts" webpage illustrates one effective approach to providing easy access to important information (Web Search: "Xaverian Brothers High School Westwood, MA"). On the "fast facts" page in the *About Us* link, parents have access to a wealth of important information, including facts about school history, enrollment information, academic quality indicators, extracurricular opportunities, athletic accomplishments, and service and faith formation programs.

Pacelli Catholic Schools provides another good example of how to present information in a format that is quickly read and powerfully impactful (Web Search: "Pacelli Catholic Schools Stevens Point, WI"). The Pacelli Catholic Schools serve a K-12 student population. Important information is shared on their website in the About Us link using a by-the-numbers infographic.

Using Your School Motto in Your Communications Plan

Another way to quickly provide people with a great deal of important information about your school is through a well-crafted school motto. An effective motto makes clear, in a few words or a short phrase, the *essence* of your school community. It answers the question of *why* your school exists. It is a powerful tool for framing your story and how you tell it to your stakeholders and prospective parents.

Drawing on their review of literature from the corporate world, Kohli, Leuthesser, and Suri (2007) make several recommendations regarding mottos and slogans, including:

- Focus on the long-term to ensure your motto stays relevant
- Highlight your institution's strengths
- Link your motto to your institution's brand (symbol, story, location)
- Make your motto memorable and repeatable
- Use your motto regularly

Your school's motto ought to sum up your vision for your graduates in a memorable way that strengthens your school's brand and conveys its purpose. Moreover, the motto ought to communicate your school's commitment to your students' intellectual, physical, and spiritual growth over time. Figures 6.4 and 6.5 provide examples of effective school mottos that reflect these characteristics.

Figure 6.4 Mercy High School Motto (Omaha, NE)

Mercy HIGH SCHOOL
Omaha, Nebraska

Where Mercy Girls Become Women of Mercy

Figure 6.5 Creighton Preparatory School Motto (Omaha, NE)

In the examples in Figures 6.4 and 6.5, the word *mercy* and the phrase *men for others* call to mind many of Jesus's sayings in the Gospels related to being compassionate and helping others. These two mottos are aspirational statements–results-oriented and responsive to their schools' vision for their graduates after graduation. These two mottos are memorable, and they communicate themes of human maturation and spiritual growth in a compelling way.

Both mottos also build on the schools' brand. For example, the Mercy motto includes the name of the school. The Creighton Prep motto is a well-known characteristic of Jesuit schools coined by a former superior general of the Jesuits.

Collaboratively Developing Your Communications Plan

Catholic school leaders are faced with a multitude of challenges in leading a Catholic school. The job requires so much of those whose formal training is typically limited to issues of academic and instructional leadership. For example, Catholic school leaders are also responsible for faith leadership, financial planning, enrollment management, and all the other day-to-day emergencies that occupy leaders' time. Clearly, leaders of Catholic schools do not have time to develop an effective communications strategy by themselves. This is why it is so important to distribute responsibility for communications issues and to engage the talent, skills, and leadership of others.

Designating a Director of Communications

I recommend that Catholic school leaders designate a director of communications. In schools that are well-resourced, this position might be a stand-alone hire. In smaller schools with more limited resources, a position like this might be embedded into a teaching position for which release time is provided. Table 6.3 provides some details about typical roles and responsibilities that might be assigned to a director of communications.

Table 6.3 Director of Communications Roles & Responsibilities

Director of Communications Role	Examples of Responsibilities
Monitor social media channels	■ Engage in chats ■ Answer questions ■ Share content ■ Review content ■ Monitor analytics
Talk with faculty to develop social media content	■ Acquire content including ◆ Text ◆ Images ◆ Video
Update and maintain content for the school's website	■ Ensure that content is current and relevant ■ Ensure that the school's motto and mission are adequately represented ■ Monitor data regarding website performance including analytics
Utilize the principles of inbound marketing	■ Develop content that inspires prospective parents to visit the school's website or school campus ■ Provide information related to school choice drivers for parents

A director of communications can manage and monitor your school's most important communications tool, your website. The website audit tool in Table 6.4 can be helpful to your director of communications as he or she takes stock of how your school's website tells your school's story. The website audit tool draws attention to some of the most important elements of an effective school website. By identifying those areas that require attention, a director of communications will be able to make informed decisions about how to focus efforts to make the school's online presence more engaging and inviting to prospective families and others who want to learn more about your school's story.

Table 6.4 Website Audit Tool for Catholic Schools

Criterion	Not Visible	Plan in Place to Add	Visible & High-Quality
Your school's name is prominently displayed on your school website.			
Your school's website clearly identifies your school as a Catholic school, and if appropriate, a school of a sponsoring religious order.			
Your school's crest or logo is prominently displayed on your school website.			
Your school's motto is prominently displayed on your school website.			
Your school's mission statement is prominently displayed on your landing page or is one click away from the landing page.			
Your school's website includes links for others to follow your school on popular social media channels.			
Totals →			

Enlisting & Equipping Parents to Tell Your School's Story

In Catholic schools, we recognize that parents are the primary educators of their children (*Catechism of the Catholic Church*, 1993). Catholic schools partner with families to help students grow and develop. Parents have a unique perspective on how their children experience your school, and they can become your most effective advocates and storytellers.

However, building a broad network of supportive and engaged parents doesn't happen by accident! Building a strong network requires an intentional effort that is grounded in dialogue and encounter. Some of this network building can occur organically; for example, during athletic events, assemblies, and at other school functions that parents naturally attend. When you encounter parents in these settings, you have an opportunity to transmit and reinforce your school's values, charisms, and compelling story so they can share your school's story with others. At the same time, it is also helpful to engage current and former parents in a more structured way to assist with your school marketing and communications efforts.

Consider which parents would be most adept at telling your school's story. Examples include those who have had multiple children attend your school and who themselves attended your school. An effective communications effort will also enlist parents from a broad cross-section of your school community to tell your school's story to others.

Meeting with selected parents regularly as a coordinated team of storytellers can help ensure the consistency of the messaging you seek to convey to the greater community. Once your parent communications partners are ready to share your story, there are many ways they can naturally assist with your communications efforts. I list a few examples to prime your thinking:

- Parent storytellers can speak at Mass about the Catholic schools their children attend, especially during Catholic Schools Week.
- Parents can provide written content for your school newsletter or social media feeds on a regular basis, sharing highlights and information that showcase various facets of your school community that would be of interest to other parents.
- Parents can provide testimonials on your school's website and in your media campaigns.
- Parent storytellers can meet with prospective parents who are discerning enrolling their children in your school to assist them with their discernment process (Burke, 2016).
- Parent storytellers can participate in outreach, such as following up with prospective parents who have inquired about the school through e-mail or on the website (Burke, 2016).

While parent engagement in your communications efforts can be very helpful, it is important to ensure consistency in your messaging. That is why it is helpful to provide parents with a brochure or one-sheet summary of key talking points that they can study and use when they encounter others in a storytelling capacity. Table 6.5 presents some examples of what a parent talking points brochure might contain.

Table 6.5 Examples of Content for a Parent Talking Points Brochure

Names of high schools or colleges your alumni are attending
High school graduation rate
Four-year college acceptance rates for your graduates
The value of faith formation as evidenced by student testimonials and graduate profiles, number of service hours, student groups related to faith and service
Number of athletic teams
Number of co-curricular activities
Number of advanced placement or international baccalaureate courses
Transportation options available for students
Affordability information
Student to teacher ratio
Number of priests, deacons, and religious working in the school
Race and ethnicity demographic figures for students and staff
Religious denomination demographics for students
Student testimonials related to a safe and welcoming environment

Earlier in this chapter, we examined the benefits of connecting themes in your school's story with the key decision-making priorities parents focus on to make school enrollment decisions. Remember that in Tables 6.1 and 6.2, I identified some parent decision-making priorities for school choice. As you develop your talking points brochure for use with your parent communications partners, be sure to focus on research-based parent decision-making priorities.

Enlisting & Equipping Students to Tell Your School's Story

Your students can also be important storytellers! For example, you can invite current students to share videos, pictures, and other content to be posted on your school's website. Students can speak at open houses, and they can interact with children and parents who are interested in learning more about your school. Secondary school student ambassadors can visit feeder elementary schools, providing their perspectives on what life is like as a student in your school (Burke, 2015).

Like parents, students need to be coached on how to tell your school's story. Students do best with prepared talking points, and providing students with talking points will help ensure both the quality and accuracy of the story they tell. Additionally, we recommend that you provide students opportunities to practice and rehearse their storytelling by engaging them in simulated meetings with other students posing as prospective students and parents. During these simulated meetings, provide coaching for your student storytellers. If your student storytellers will provide tours of your school to prospective students and parents, provide them with a pre-planned route with defined stops and talking points for each stop. I provide some examples of talking points for a school tour in Table 6.6.

Table 6.6 Talking Points for Student-led Tours

School Tour Stop	Examples of Talking Points
School Chapel	■ Say a few words about the saint to whom the chapel is consecrated and the relationship of the saint to our school's story ■ Share a story about how you have used the chapel
Main Office Suite	■ Describe when and how students might engage with school administrators (keep it positive)
Cafeteria	■ Describe lunch options for students
Typical Classroom	■ Mention the average number of students in a class ■ Talk about special features such as technology or type of desks ■ Share about a teacher who had a positive impact on you ■ Share your impressions of what it is like to be a student in a classroom ■ Describe typical homework expectations
Library/Digital Media Center	■ Describe resources available to students ■ Share a story about how you benefited from the library/media center
Gymnasium	■ Discuss opportunities for athletics and physical development ■ Describe the link between athletics, physical development, and your school's story
Fine & Performing Arts Center	■ Describe some of the productions students have put on recently ■ Share about your experience in a production or your experience of attending a production

Remember that prospective students and parents are most interested in what the school experience might be like for them. This is why it is important that student ambassadors focus on telling the story of *their* experiences in your school. You ought to identify student storytellers who will be able to passionately share the essence of their positive experiences in the school community with others.

Evaluating Your Communications Plan by Creating a Feedback Loop

To maximize the effectiveness of your communications plan, you need to evaluate your plan. School leaders need to be intentional about evaluating their school's communications strategies through the use of a feedback loop. A feedback loop is an intentional and structured process of gathering data to determine if your message is being received, understood, and acted upon by your stakeholders. Figure 6.6 outlines how a thoughtfully developed evaluative practice can close the feedback loop and help school leaders make data-based decisions about the communications process.

Figure 6.6 Closing Your School's Communications Plan Feedback Loop

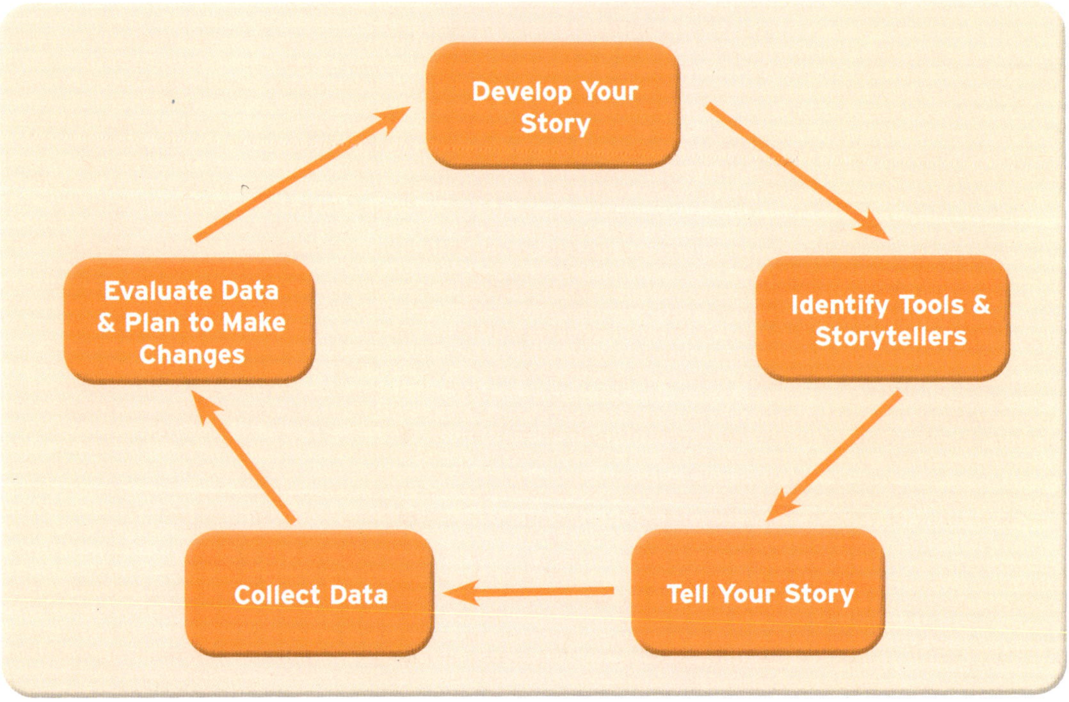

Develop Your Story → Identify Tools & Storytellers → Tell Your Story → Collect Data → Evaluate Data & Plan to Make Changes → Develop Your Story

To collect data about the effectiveness of your communications plan, you need to develop strategies to determine if people are listening to your message, if people are understanding your message, and if people are taking action based on your message. One way to focus your data collection process is to focus on what people are hearing and what people are doing. For example, ask parents and local community members what they are hearing about your school and then follow up and ask where they heard the information. Additionally, your school's director of communications can monitor local media reports and social media channels for emergent themes related to your school.

To evaluate if people are taking action based on your message, set up analytics such as tracking the number of website visits before and after a communications campaign and the number of other incoming contacts your marketing, communications, and enrollment management staff receive. The ultimate goal of a good school communications plan is to bring people to your website and to your school, especially prospective parents, prospective students, and potential benefactors. By monitoring inbound communications, you can determine the effectiveness of specific communications strategies and use those strategies that prove to encourage the most action by those who listen to and understand your message.

Conclusion

The title of this book is *Writing a New Story for Catholic Schools*. Framing the work that you do at your school as being a storyteller is an innovative way for you and others on your team to conceptualize your role in leading your school forward. By embracing some of the innovative communications practices that are outlined in this chapter, you and your stakeholders will become dynamic storytellers, adept at sharing the good news of your school and inspiring others to want to be a part of your school community.

In the next part of this book, Fr. Simonds will draw together all of the ideas and innovative practices shared in this book. His concluding chapter includes templates that you can use to implement the practices shared in this book. There is a sample planning template for each chapter of this book, as well as a blank template that you can copy and fill in yourself.

Notes

PART THREE

Conclusion

Thomas A. Simonds, S.J., Ed.D.

CHAPTER SEVEN:
Publishing Your School's New Story

My hope in sharing this book with you is that you and your school team can learn from the past successes of Catholic education and create a new success story for your Catholic school. When the need for Catholic schools was deeply felt by the Catholic community in the 1800s and 1900s, community members worked together to build an amazing school system. While our situation today is much changed, Catholic schools still provide a unique opportunity for student faith formation and life preparation that is not available in any other type of school.

Using this book, you and your team can enhance the affordability of your Catholic school through the use of new school models, by accessing state and federal resources, and through active advocacy for parental choice in education. I believe that if you work on the affordability goal first, you will be able to build school enrollment right away.

Equally important is the goal of adopting new program and curricular models that meet parent priorities. Many parents still desire a different type of education for their children, and Catholic schools can meet their desires through creative new initiatives and collaboration.

A number of the new school models and initiatives that Dr. Ron Fussell and I have advocated for in this book hinge on providing convenient and affordable transportation options for students and their families. Student transportation to school is a public service that has been approved for use by all students in local communities, including students who attend private schools. Working together with local leaders and community members, you and your team can put in place new and affordable transportation options for your students.

The ideas and practices Dr. Ron Fussell shared in Chapters Five and Six for recruiting and hiring faculty, and for developing a new communications plan, are relatively easy changes to make at your school. Changes in hiring practices and the development of a new communications plan primarily require access to the ideas and the will to implement the ideas. We have provided the new ideas and encourage you to take the next step and innovate at your school by hiring new and effective storytellers and by telling your story in new and imaginative ways.

To assist you with developing and writing your school's new story, I have provided planning templates in this chapter for you to use. The first planning template is blank, and you are welcome to make copies of this page and use it for your own planning process.

I have also provided a planning template related to each topic in Chapters Two through Six in this book. These completed planning templates will help you brainstorm how to address a particular need or goal at your school. I suggest that you decide on one focus area to begin with and build out the publication of your school's story from that one focus area. As I mentioned above, I suggest you start with reviewing Chapters Two and Three and focus on addressing the affordability issue. If you can make progress in the key area of school affordability, work on other needs and goals will follow.

In addition to guiding the development and telling of your school's new story, the planning templates can also be used to determine professional development needs and to assess the work of your leadership team. Once you decide on your goals, then you can consider if your staff needs additional knowledge and skills to accomplish the goals. Also, by setting clear goals and timelines for innovation, assessment will be naturally built into your innovation process.

We pray that you move forward to publish a new story for your Catholic school with the wisdom and graces given by the Holy Spirit. Working together with your team, your parents, your students, and all your stakeholders, a new way forward is possible!

Notes

Blank Planning Template

You have permission to make copies of this page and use this blank planning template as you apply the ideas and best practices from this book at your school.

NSBECS Benchmark*	Focus Area	Three-Year Goals
		Year One: Explore Options
		End of Year One: Reassess & Rewrite Year Two & Year Three Goals
		Year Two: Choose & Develop an Option
		Year Three: Implement the Option

* National Standards and Benchmarks for Effective Catholic Elementary and Secondary Schools. See *www.catholicschoolstandards.org* for more information.

Sample Planning Templates

Enhancing Affordability

NSBECS Benchmark*	Focus Area	Three-Year Goals
10.1 10.3	Affordable Schools (see Chapter Two)	**Year One:** Explore new school models that address affordability; for example, talk with your local education agency (LEA) about support for student transportation, consider development of a network of grade schools, and explore corporate partnership options.
		Year Two: Adopt a new school model that addresses affordability and fits your context and engage in planning.
		Year Three: Implement the new school model to enhance affordability of your school for students and families.

* National Standards and Benchmarks for Effective Catholic Elementary and Secondary Schools.
See *www.catholicschoolstandards.org* for more information.

Developing Broad Support

NSBECS Benchmark	Focus Area	Three-Year Goals
10.3	Broadly Supported Schools (see Chapter Three)	**Year One:** Explore new strategies to broaden support for your school; for example, advocacy for school vouchers, advocacy for scholarship granting organizations (SGOs) and state scholarship tax credits, advocacy support for your school from local unions, and assistance available from a third-party provider to develop a plan to access state and federal educational resources for your school.
		Year Two: Choose and develop a new strategy to broaden support for your school.
		Year Three: Implement the new strategy to broaden support for your school and enhance your school's affordability.

Choosing New Focus Points

NSBECS Benchmark	Focus Area	Three-Year Goals
4.2 6.4	Networked Schools (see Chapter Four)	**Year One:** Determine what would motivate your stakeholders to support your school by scanning the environment and by using informal polling. Also consider how your school's location and Catholic identity can be attractive pieces of your story to share with your stakeholders.
		Year Two: Discern new focus points for your school based on scanning and polling and plan for implementation; for example, a dual language curriculum, a STEM curriculum, or a discipleship curriculum.
		Year Three: Implement new curricular and program models that will motivate stakeholder commitment to your school.

Hiring New Faculty Storytellers

NSBECS Benchmark	Focus Area	Three-Year Goals
2.5 2.7 3.4 4.5 11.3	Hiring Faculty to Tell Your School's New Story (see Chapter Five)	**Year One:** Develop a coordinated faculty recruitment, hiring, and professional development process (see Figure 5.1).
		Year Two: Put in place the pieces you need for your recruitment and hiring process to function; for example, develop relationships with Catholic colleges and universities, develop relationships with Catholic seminaries, explore alternative teacher preparation models, and develop a planned hiring process.
		Year Three: Begin using your coordinated faculty recruitment, hiring, and professional development process.

Developing a New Communications Plan

NSBECS Benchmark	Focus Area	Three-Year Goals
10.7 13.1	Telling Your School's New Story with a Communications Plan (see Chapter Six)	**Year One:** Evaluate your current communications plan, including resources allocated; for example, staff assigned, practices used, and effectiveness of current practices.
		Year Two: Based on your evaluation of your communications plan, set goals for improvement and plan for acquisition of the necessary resources; for example, increase staff assigned to communications, revise your website, leverage social media, and increase parent involvement in your communications process.
		Year Three: Address the goals for improvement designed to improve your communications plan.

Notes

REFERENCES

Burke, M. (2015, Fall). Elementary and secondary school partnerships strengthen enrollment. *Momentum*, 46(4), 54-55.

Burke, M. (2016, Spring). Enrollment success: Recruiting one student at a time. *Momentum*, 47(2), 54-55.

Catechism of the Catholic Church. (1993). Libreria Editrice Vaticana.

Congregation for Catholic Education. (1982). *Lay Catholic in schools: Witnesses to faith*. https://www.vatican.va/roman_curia/congregations/ccatheduc/documents/rc_con_ccatheduc_doc_19821015_lay-catholics_en.html

Congregation for Catholic Education. (2014). *Educating today and tomorrow: A renewing passion*. http://www.vatican.va/roman_curia/congregations/ccatheduc/documents/rc_con_ccatheduc_doc_20140407_educare-oggi-e-domani_en.html

Cook, T. J. (2015). *Charism and culture: Cultivating Catholic identity in Catholic schools*. National Catholic Educational Association.

Cremin, L. A. (Ed.). (1979). *The republic and the school: Horace Mann on the education of free men* (10th ed.). Teacher's College Press.

EdChoice. (2017). *2017 schooling in America survey.* www.edchoice.org

EdChoice. (2018). *2018 schooling in America survey.* www.edchoice.org

EdChoice. (2019). *2019 schooling in America survey.* www.edchoice.org

(FADICA) Foundations and Donors Interested in Catholic Activities. (2018). *The Catholic school choice: Understanding the perspectives of parents*. https://www.fadica.org/images/initiatives/The-Catholic-School-Choice_2018.pdf

Ford, P. L. (Ed.). (1962). *The New England primer*. Teacher's College Press. (Original work published 1897)

Gorn, E. J. (Ed.). (1998). *The McGuffey readers: Selections from the 1879 edition.* Bedford/St. Martin's.

Kohli, C., Leuthesser, L., Suri, R. (2007). Got slogan? Guidelines for creating effective slogans. *Business Horizons*, (50)3, 415-422.

LeBeau, B. F. (2000). *Religion in America to 1865*. New York University Press.

McDonald, D. (2020, Spring). Religious liberty before the Supreme Court. *Momentum*, 46-47. Hope and opportunities for education choice in 2020. *Momentum*, 51(2), 32-33.

McDonald, D., & Schultz, M. (2020). *U.S. Catholic elementary and secondary schools 2019-2020*. National Catholic Educational Association.

Melley, K. B. (2019). Sowing the NSBECS: Professional development approaches for sustained Catholic school change. *Journal of Catholic Education*, 22(1), 202-206. https://doi.org/10.15365/joce.2201142019

(NCES) National Center for Education Statistics. (2019). *Digest of education statistics 2018*. www.nces.ed.gov

Ozar, L. A., & Weitzel-O'Neill, P. (Eds.). (2012). *National standards and benchmarks for effective Catholic elementary and secondary schools*. http://catholicschoolstandards.org

Online Etymology Dictionary. (n.d.) https://www.etymonline.com/

Peterson, S. M. (2020, Spring). Hope and opportunities for education choice in 2020. *Momentum*, 32-33. Hope and opportunities for education choice in 2020. *Momentum*, 51(2), 32-33.

Sevell+Sevell, Inc. (2021). *How much time should someone spend on your website?* https://www.sevell.com/news/how-much-time-should-someone-spend-your-website#:~:text=Research%20shows%20the%20average%20time,website%20is%20about%2045%20seconds.

Walch, T. (2003). *Parish school: American Catholic parochial education from colonial times to the present*. National Catholic Educational Association.

AUTHOR NOTES

Fr. Thomas A. Simonds, S.J., Ed.D.

Father Tom Simonds is a Catholic priest and a member of the Society of Jesus. He is currently Timms Professor of Humanities at Creighton University in Omaha, NE and oversees the undergraduate core curriculum. He has held a number of leadership positions in Catholic secondary schools including principal and school trustee. Father Simonds is the author of 18 articles on Catholic educational issues. He has authored two books: *School Violence Prevention Workbook* and *Advent and Christmas Reflections for Teachers*, and he has co-authored one book: *Your School's Catholic Identity: Name It, Claim It, and Build on It*. All these books are available from the National Catholic Educational Association. Father Simonds can be contacted at *tsimonds@creighton.edu*.

Ronald D. Fussell, Ed.D.

Dr. Fussell is a core faculty member in Creighton's innovative educational leadership programs, where he serves as the director of Catholic school leadership and teaches courses for aspiring Catholic school leaders. Prior to joining the education department faculty at Creighton, Dr. Fussell was the associate superintendent of schools for the Diocese of Manchester, where he led innovative efforts to improve diocesan curricula, leadership development, teacher and principal evaluation, and Catholic school identity in service to 26 schools and nearly 6,000 Catholic school students in the state of New Hampshire. A passionate advocate for Catholic education, Dr. Fussell is honored to have a national voice regarding important topics such as lay Catholic educator faith formation, Catholic school identity, and Catholic school leadership development. Dr. Fussell can be reached at *ronaldfussell@creighton.edu*.